3

Trials, Tears and Triumph

Trials, Tears and Triumph

Dale Evans Rogers

Fleming H. Revell Company
Old Tappan, New Jersey

Unless otherwise identified, Scripture quotations are from the King James Version of the Bible.

Scripture quotations identified LB are from The Living Bible, Copyright © 1971 by Tyndale House Publishers, Wheaton, Illinois 60187.

Excerpts from *Believe!* by Richard M. DeVos with Charles Paul Conn are Copyright © 1975 by Richard M. DeVos. Published by Fleming H. Revell Company. Used by permission.

"Victory in Defeat" by Edwin Markham is reprinted by permission of Mrs. Virgil Markham.

Library of Congress Cataloging in Publication Data

Rogers, Dale Evans
    Trials, tears and triumph.

    1. Rogers, Dale Evans. 2. Christian biography
California. I. Title.
BR1725.R63A324   209'.2'4 [B]   76–51293
ISBN 0–8007–0847–4

BY *Dale Evans Rogers*

Contents

Introduction to The King's Highway

Having spent some years of my life in show business, I know well what show-biz people mean when they speak of "the road." The road is their school of hard knocks, in which they serve their apprenticeship before they hit the theaters of the big cities or prime time on TV.

It's a hard road and a tough life. It means one-night stands in dreary small-town halls and theaters that are freezing in winter and stifling in summer, putting up at third-rate hotels, sleeping on buses or trains as they scurry from one town to the next, eating food that makes their stomachs roar in protest. One minute they are afraid they're going to die, and the next minute they're afraid they won't. And all they can do about it is to grit their teeth and hope the next town may be better.

I travel that road no longer; since I turned my life over to Jesus Christ and asked Him to send me wherever He wanted me to go, I have found another road, and I love it. I travel it for God. I even have a godly name for it.

Out here in California there is a road running from Los Angeles to San Francisco; all along it there are little white stakes or markers bearing the name of the road: *El Camino Real.* In Spanish that means "The Royal Road," or, as some of the older folks call it, "The King's Highway."

That's it! That's where I'm traveling now—a King's Highway—God's Highway—that runs all the way from Bethlehem and Nazareth and Gethsemane and Calvary to now. It is the road which Paul and the apostles walked, the road stained red by the blood of the martyrs, the road along which the seeds of the Church and the faith were dropped in the early days.

I'm never lonesome, on this Highway, as I was on the show-biz road; those early travelers walk with me like so many sainted ghosts, and I am forever hearing what Thoreau called the "sound of a different drummer"—a voice from beyond the troubled road tells me that He will be with me always, even unto the end of the road.

It wasn't easy for Paul, on *his* King's Highway. He tells us, "I have traveled many weary miles and have been often in great danger from flooded rivers, and from robbers, and from my own people, the Jews, as well as from the hands of the Gentiles . . ." (2 Corinthians 11:26 LB). It isn't as dangerous as that for me, but, as with any witness for Christ, I have been faced with rivers of criticism and ridicule that are the devil's traps, by agnostics and atheists who would give anything to rob me of my faith. There are times when I have been so exhausted that sleep would not come, so tired that I doubted I could walk another mile. There have been obstacles thrown in my path—cars stalled in snowstorms, flat tires along lonesome roads, planes delayed for hours while I fumed in airports, lost baggage, lost money, lost contacts, lost directions in strange cities—*but never lost hope or faith.*

To further complicate matters, I have had, I think, a full share of sorrow. I have lost loved ones—three children, parents, a dear brother, close friends. Death has been all around me, but—and in this *but* is my reason for and my purpose in writing this book—I have found in the God of the Highway One who has given me strength to come through these trials, who has wiped away my tears, who has given me triumph over everything the devil could throw at me.

I want to tell you about my contact with this compassionate, healing, all-powerful God.

No, it hasn't been an easy road, but I wouldn't stop walking it for anything this world could give me. I often think of that line in the Talmud which reads, "Three things are weakening: fear, sin and travel." Fear? Of course I have known fear; everyone on the face of our earth is afraid of something or someone. But I have found the perfect antidote for fear. Whenever it sticks up its ugly face I clobber it with prayer, and I have come to the place in which I fear nothing anyone can do to me. The only fear left in me is that I may let God down somewhere along the trail. Sin? I knew sin before I knew Christ, knew its danger and power, but now I walk with the Conqueror of sin, Christ Jesus, and it frightens me no more. Travel? There are more than 965 million Christians in this world, all won by traveling missionaries and witnesses of the faith, and I am driven of God that there may be more.

I travel the Highway as excited and expectant as an explorer, anxious with every passing mile that I may find some new place or heart in which to plant the seeds of forgiveness, mercy, and a new birth in God. This book is made up of excerpts from my travel diary, of my journeys hither and yon, of my ups and downs, of the problems I have discussed with seeking people (Forgive me if I am lengthy here: such meditations are part of *any* diary!) along the way. It concerns the great souls I have met, the friends I have made, the blessed challenges of coming face-to-face with those who say in their hearts that there is no God.

Nothing means more to me, as I travel this road, than the thrill of hearing someone say, "I'll walk His way from now on."

Come travel with me. Welcome aboard!

Trials, Tears and Triumph

God Bless It

It is always good to start a day or a journey or a speech or a book with a prayer; we need to stop before we start, to get our minds quieted and our thinking straight and our purpose clear. It is good to start *anything* with a "God bless it."

God, bless this diary, and keep my mind running clear. I've got so much to say and I want to say it in a language that others can understand.

Forgive me if I get my dates mixed up now and then, or if I get too busy with a lot of trivia or neglect to accentuate the positive and slow down on the negative. Please help me to walk circumspectly, as you helped Paul, not as a fool but as one ". . . wise, Redeeming the time, because the days are evil . . . understanding what the will of the Lord is" (Ephesians 5:15–17).

Our days do seem evil; we live in a degenerate age; to speak up for You in such a time, we—I—need to "put on the whole armour of God . . ." that I may ". . . be able to withstand in the evil day, and having done all, to stand. . . . And for me, that utterance may be given unto me, that I may open

my mouth boldly, to make known the mystery of the gospel"
(Ephesians 6:11–19).

May I do it Your way, Lord, not my way. Have Your way
with me. Amen.

Chicago, Illinois

Well, here I am aboard a "Proud Bird" plane at O'Hare
Airport. Had quite a fuss getting aboard. I've seen some long
boarding lines in my time, but this was one of the worst in
aviation history. I was bumped and pushed around until I
wanted to drop my bag and just hit somebody in protest.
Good old Buttermilk, my buckskin horse in our TV series,
never bounced me more and never moved faster than I
moved to make it to Gate D-9. After the battle, we sat for
a long time waiting for the plane to make up its mind
whether it was going to take off or stay on the ground. That
happens often on the road; you learn to live with it. My mom
says that this hustle and bustle at the airport reminds her of
the Scripture on the last days: ". . . many shall run to and
fro . . ." (Daniel 12:4).

It was a hectic day I spent in Chicago, on this trip. Fleming H. Revell Company, my publisher, had arranged for me
to appear on the "Chicago A.M." broadcast, to introduce my
book *Let Freedom Ring* in the area. It was supposed to be
one appearance or broadcast, but as usual it turned out to be
several interviews on and off the air.

On "Chicago A.M." I found myself chattering away with the emcee and then with a delightfully amusing and informative authority on gardening. He told me how to cultivate a sweet-potato kitchen plant. He told me to start by putting a potato (with several eyes) in a solution of weak tea, supported in a jar or container with toothpicks (I use nails). Then I should wait for about a month to begin adding water and a little occasional plant food. He said, "Plants are not human and they do not cry when they are cut, as some folks suppose, but they do make a noise. Plants are not induced to grow by a lot of sweet talk, but it does speed the growth of the one giving it." That made sense. Then he made a statement that made me blink: "Plants and humans grow only in darkness!"

It may sound like trivia, but there was nothing trivial about it. I believe it, because, as one stumbling human, I have never learned much or grown much from the flush of "light" in success and pleasure; I have learned a lot and grown a lot in my trials and tribulations and in the darkness of suffering and pain. There is great godly purpose in darkness. That's just one of the diamonds I have picked up along the road.

I rushed off for my second appearance of the day, which was at a radio luncheon broadcast. I hadn't expected this, but one of the interviewers asked me to go on for some thirty minutes, at the luncheon, with another lady who was promoting a new film. I said sure, and that was to lead me into a pretty lively discussion.

As I stepped out of the doorway onto State Street, a lady carrying one of my books asked me to be photographed with her, with me holding a copy of *Let Freedom Ring.* We were all set for the photographer to shoot when Chicago's nastiest pigeon of the year swooped down over our heads and—I had heard of this happening to others, but I never thought it would happen to me, but happen it did—all over the beautiful jacket of the book, all down the front of my new blue dress (a gift from Mom, who said she was tired of seeing me in slack suits). I shook my fist at the disappearing pigeon and blessed him with a line stolen from Flip Wilson: "The devil made you do that!" With the help of several ladies and many tissues, I made myself presentable and went on to the luncheon.

What I met at the luncheon was one of those pert, pretty, and very personable young "liberated" women—the mother of six children, a very free-thinking young lady who was quite "hep" about the world she was living in. I'm sure she had heard or read some of my Christian witness, and that she had been preparing herself to meet me head-on. She was in Chicago to promote a film entitled *Naked Came the Stranger.* Frankly, I felt a bit like a stranger living in another world from hers when she began to explain the contents of the book and the film. With an almost childlike incredulity, she wondered how anyone could question their raucously sexy "values." When the interviewer asked her what she thought of Mrs. Betty Ford's now famous remarks about trial marriage and the relationships of young people, she almost exploded with admiration and praise for our First Lady's understanding and acceptance of present "facts of life."

Then the interviewer asked me to give my reaction to Mrs. Ford's statements, and I lowered the boom.

I said, "I was disappointed. I very much admire Mrs. Ford's courage and willingness to share that courage with other women afflicted with breast cancer; I think she is a very warm, sincere, and attractive woman. But, considering the pressures put upon the American home and family—our high and climbing divorce rate, the rise in crimes of rape, murder, and robbery—I thought some of her other remarks unfortunate. Neither do I agree with her on abortion. But, as Ann Landers says, I'm a square, so who cares what I think?"

Yes, I'm a square—but I still have the right to believe what I will and the right to say it, just as Mrs. Ford says it. But when she indicated that maybe by living together on a trial basis, there would be fewer divorces, I wonder if she considers the fact that there might be fewer marriages and possibly more unwanted children that way. Sometimes the best laid plans for contraception fail. Terminated affairs are traumatic experiences, and when children are involved, the children suffer the worst traumas of all. That seems disgustingly unfair to me.

I am saying this in the realization that prior to my real encounter with Jesus Christ twenty-eight years ago, my own life was far from perfect and certainly questionable on many counts. But whatever mess I found myself in, I never tried to justify the sin in my life by saying, "Oh, times have changed and we just have to accept it and live with it." We do *not* have to accept it as "moral" or as the highest ideal of life. I believe we have to deal with it as the Bible deals with it. The Bible tells me that there is always a payday when we are called to account for going against God's moral law, when we pay one by one for the sins we have committed two by two. It has always worked out just as He said it would work out and it always will, regardless of our high-sounding, free-thinking, so-called new morality.

Facts of life? Crime is a fact of life. Adultery is a fact of life. Human lust and greed and selfishness are facts of life, too—but we do not have to buy any of this sad package if we don't want to.

"Do your own thing," said the young lady. Do it, and if it doesn't work out, then simply split up and go your own way when it is no longer "meaningful." Tell me this. How is any sexual relation meaningful when there is no real commitment, no decent love involved?

En Route to Los Angeles, California

I keep thinking about that gal's way of life, and mine.

Every time I have let down the barriers of God's moral standards in my life, I have been left dispirited and disappointed in myself and experienced an inner yearning to be stronger in my convictions of right and wrong, and to have the courage to stand by my convictions, even if I have to stand alone. So stand, says the Bible!

Not until I surrendered my will to God through Christ did I have the will to live and stand by my convictions and by His help, for twenty-eight years, I have walked a pretty straight line. Oh, sure, I "put on a happy face" to the world in my preconversion days, but inside my heart ached with failure to measure up to the standards I had been taught and that I knew to be God's standards. Sin—or missing God's mark—never, *never* made me happy; it always left me with a sense of shame and insecurity.

I suppose that some of these modern "live-in" arrangements (something my generation didn't do) *do* culminate in marriage, that those involved do discover that they love each other and they want some surety, some sort of contract, to protect their love. If they had only known that earlier, if they had learned to like the good qualities that they had in common, marriage *then* would not have been a risk to their relationships. Somehow, it seems that when there is a contract between two people, they both try harder. Cool reason is far better than impulsiveness in the love-and-marriage department. While the live-in idea never occurred to me in my younger days, I would have spared myself and others a lot of worry and heartache if I had been less impulsive.

I know that there are a lot of people who disagree with me in all of this. Someone has said that there is no one so sanctimonious as a reformed drunk, and some who knew me in my early years might be tempted to say the same thing about my "puritanical" stance since becoming a Christian. Mind you, I say *becoming* a Christian. Christianity, you know, is a process of *becoming*. You may never reach perfection as a Christian, but remember that Christians are no more than sinners who have been saved by the atoning blood and grace of Jesus Christ, and as they come more and more to understand that, they become more and more Christian, but never perfect Christians.

No, this "new morality" which prompts the live-in shambles is neither new nor moral: it goes all the way back to poor old Eve in the Garden. Why didn't Eve—why couldn't Eve —tell that snake to buzz off? It was a tyranny of the flesh that led her to put her own "new" morality in the place of God's morality. And you may recall the story of Abraham and Sarah. When Sarah was unable to give Abraham the son and heir for which he longed, she sent him to have a son named Ishmael by her maidservant Hagar. God made of Ishmael's descendants "a great nation" (Genesis 21:18)—but, in the eyes of the Jews, an outlaw nation because Ishmael was born outside the marriage relation with Sarah. It was a divided sonship, and there has been conflict between the sons of Ishmael and the sons of Isaac (the son of Abraham and Sarah, born when they were very old) ever since. Some Bible scholars see the beginnings of the endless Middle East wars in all of this. Isaac, born in wedlock, was the true "son of promise" (*see* Genesis 17:19; 18:10). Ishmael was not the one in whom the seed of God's own people was planted. Poor Ishmael! He paid dearly for the behavior of his parents.

So why don't we wise up and take God's way in the first place?

To get back to the lady at the luncheon for a minute—she asked me two other questions. Didn't I know that in countries where the live-in arrangement is generally accepted there is hardly any rape? Yes, I had heard that—but had she ever heard of the rape of decency? My God demands not indecent lust but decency. My Bible makes it pretty plain to me that we are to worship not the creature but the Creator, not to put our trust in princes or in anyone who defies Him and His laws. He did *not* create us to become slaves to the flesh.

She asked me, "How can you think that it is fair for the man to have all the affairs he wants and be considered merely a swinger when if a woman does the same thing she is considered a bum?" When did I ever say that, or even think it? Never! I said to her that according to the New Testament, God is no respecter of persons (*see* Colossians 3:25) and that in His sight—as well as in mine—the man is just as guilty as the woman. And isn't it within the realm of possibility that chastity is more to be expected of the woman for the simple reason that as child bearer of the race she has a divine responsibility? She didn't seem interested in responsibility.

Toward the end, I asked her, "Look, isn't there anything

in the world but sex?" She eyeballed me with "What?" I
pitied her. Can any sensible man or woman live a life in
which there is nothing but sex?

I suppose that a lot of people would say that this woman
was being "artistically realistic" in promoting *Naked Came
the Stranger,* but if that's what it is, thank you, I'd rather be
unartistic. And what's realistic about spending even an hour
of your time watching a porn movie that degrades sex into
filth?

At a hotel in Minneapolis, Roy and I watched one of those
cable TV porn movies. Never have I been more bored and
disgusted. I fell asleep halfway through the film. I know—
some will say that was because I am no longer young. None-
sense! Even when I was young, pornography always bored
and embarrassed me. I see no art in any of it; it is pandering
to the lowest morality in the world, and to the lowest breed
of men. It takes no talent to be dirty. That movie made me
ashamed of the producer and the director as well as the
actors and actresses in the film. I have been told, "You
should see some of these box-office movies that have such
long lines out front." Okay. I saw one—and seeing it blew
my chance for a badly needed full-night's sleep and I woke
up the next morning asking God to forgive me for wasting
my time looking at such garbage.

To cluck-cluck at such obscenity is not enough. A Christian should have no part in it, even as a spectator. He would
do better to get in the long lines out front to see such films

as *The Sound of Music, Benjie,* and *The Other Side of the Mountain.* He would do better to get in the lines waiting to see John "Duke" Wayne's movies (Duke may be a little on the salty side and too violent, but comparing even his films with the one we saw on cable TV is like comparing a clear mountain stream with a sewer, Duke's epithets notwithstanding).

I sang and witnessed at the Jesus rally that night in Chicago, and it was like stepping out of a dark, smelly cellar into the sunlight. I breathed and lived again in the company of a crowd clean and Christ-conscious. I almost forgot all the interviews I had been through that day—but there had to be one more in which a Chicago newspaperman told me that he, too, was surprised and dismayed at my remarks about Mrs. Ford. He said, "You know, Dale, you sounded like Mrs. Ford yourself when you said, 'At one time in my life I would have been a good candidate for Women's Lib because I had been badly put down by a man.' I think he meant that I sounded like Mrs. Ford because I was forthright about what I think now as against what I thought in my earlier years. As so often happens, he did not quote the rest of what I had said, which was, "I'm glad there wasn't a Women's Lib then." I further explained how God had revolutionized my thinking as a woman when I gave my life to Him and how He had shown me the privilege, honor, and dignity of being a woman as God ordained it in the first place.

Home, in Bed

It's about 3 A.M. now; this is one of those nights when even counting sheep won't put me to sleep. I keep going over the interviews of that hectic day in Chicago, over and over and over, and I think of the smartest things I might have said, and didn't. I'm told that some of the most brilliant people in the world do that, so it doesn't particularly bother me; what bothers me is that I'm tired to death and can't sleep. But I'll go on doing it, as long as I can put one foot ahead of the other. Once committed to Jesus Christ, you keep walking until you drop. I'm long past the point of no return in my commitment to Him; as long as there is opportunity, I will give my witness—no matter what it costs.

I get in a word for Christ even in our rodeos and state and county fair shows, and there have been some complaints about that from folks who say that people come to our shows "not to hear you preach but to be entertained." We do not mean to preach sermons in our shows, ever, but we do feel that a verbal or musical salute to God and our country is not out of place anywhere in this land of the free. Their criticism doesn't make me mad anymore; I expect it, for Jesus tells me it will happen, and the Christian has to learn to live with it.

As a matter of fact, I would be uneasy and worried if I didn't get criticism; that would be an indication that I wasn't getting through to my critics. As a good preacher said once, "Nobody kicks a dead horse!"

The Lord has just given me a new song to sing! It goes like this:

Are you willing to follow the Lord?
When the way of the Saviour is hard?
And the path is so rugged and narrow. . . .
    Are you willing to follow the Lord?
Are you willing to challenge the crowd,
When a wound to someone is allowed?
Can you tell them to love one another?
    Are you willing to follow the Lord?
Jesus said, "Deny yourself; take up your cross and follow
    Me."
But you'll never walk alone;
Leading the way He'll always be.—
If you're willing to follow the Lord,
Then some day you will reap the reward
Of the robe and the crown that He promised—
    Are you willing to follow the Lord?

I am.

Dallas, Texas

Travel is a weird and wonderful mixture of fear and faith, comfort and catastrophe, disappointment and happy surprises, peace and anger—and a lot of love and laughter. You never know what lies in wait for you just around the corner, or at the next airport.

While reading the Book of Job the other day, I came across something that fine old sufferer said that jolted me: "The thing which I greatly feared is come upon me . . ." (Job 3:25). It jolted, because it has just happened to me.

For years, I have had a frightening, recurring dream. (Why is it that when we dream, it is so often about something frightening?) In this dream I am standing alone at midnight in a strange city, with no money, no credit cards, without a friend within a thousand miles. I've forgotten the name of the hotel at which I am supposed to stay.

Recently it happened for real.

Now the Lord is teaching me many things, one of which is to "take heed, lest ye fall" (*see* 1 Corinthians 10:12), especially when I become too judgmental of others. For instance, I often became impatient and irritated with my dear mother, who has a habit of saying, at home and away from home, "Dale, where is my purse? I've lost it." She is forever losing it—and finding it, and it was hard for me to understand why she couldn't remember what she did with it. Now I know how it feels, myself.

Monday and Tuesday, I was with Roy on location for his movie *McIntosh and T.J.* near Lubbock, Texas. On Wednesday, I left for a singing-witnessing engagement near DuBois, Pennsylvania. When I changed planes in Dallas, an American Airlines publicity man drove me to the airport and saw me through security, where I walked through the electric eye and proved to the inspectors that I had no guns, knives, or bombs on my person. I sat down near the boarding area to await the takeoff. I plopped my large red carrying bag and my large pocketbook at my feet, and proceeded to lose myself in an exciting magazine article.

All of a sudden my flight was called, and I grabbed up the carrying case and the precious magazine and rushed out to the plane. I found my seat and nodded to a nice young man who came to sit beside me, hoping against hope that he'd be still and let me finish reading my story. We taxied out on the runway. While we were waiting for the takeoff someone touched my shoulder, and I looked up into the eyes of a very compassionate young stewardess who broke it to me gently: "Mrs. Rogers, your purse is at the ticket counter." I fumbled around my feet and all over the seat—and sure enough, the purse wasn't there. I nearly had a stroke. In that purse were my airline tickets for the entire trip, my credit cards, my car keys, and cash to the amount of $347! Not one red cent did this absentminded cowgirl have to her name, nor did I have any identification to claim my bag at Pittsburgh, where I was stay overnight at a hotel.

I must have turned a pasty white, for the young man sitting beside me did his best to assure me that I needn't worry: "Your purse and everything in it are safe at the airline office; it will arrive in Pittsburgh early tomorrow morning, at the latest." My plane for DuBois was to leave Pittsburgh at 1:00 P.M. the next day, but in my heart I doubted that I would be on it; the purse would never reach me in time. On top of it all, I didn't have the name of the DuBois pastor who was to meet me at the airport—and I didn't have a dime to call anybody to find out where to go!

I sat there thinking of something I had said a day or two before. I was asked to do an interview giving my reactions to Roy's movie "off the cuff"—which meant without any preparation and without a script. It was a promotional gimmick for which I wasn't prepared, and as we walked toward the cameras one of the group said, "We won't bug you by watching you, Dale. We don't want to make you nervous." I laughed and said, "Oh, nothing makes me nervous." What I meant was that the Lord had cured me of my old *performing* nervousness; as we settled in our chairs before the cameras, Roy's producer, Tim Penland, smiled at me and said, "Nothing gets to you, does it Dale?"

"Oh, yes, some things do—but not performing," I replied. I sat there eating those words as the plane zoomed up into the air, almost beside myself and almost getting up and shouting, "Stop the plane; I want to get off!"

That young fellow sitting beside me didn't seem flustered at all; he was as cool as a cucumber about it all. At first I wanted to shoot him. Of course *he* wasn't worried; he didn't lose his purse. I cooled off a bit when he told me that there were very frequent flights by American Airlines between Dallas and Pittsburgh, and they'd have my lost bag in my room early the next morning. He got up and brought me a flight schedule to prove it—and then he told me that he worked with American Airlines, the airline we were flying.

Whew! Someone has said that the good Lord protects drunks and babies; now I know that He protects absent-minded, middle-aged women, too. Thank You, God, for putting that young man next to me on that plane.

I thought it would be nice if he would just go with me to the hotel and explain my predicament, but I didn't dare to ask him; that seemed just too much. But I didn't have to ask him because in the next split second he explained that he would do just that. Thanks again, Lord.

His brother met us at the baggage claim and looked at me in deep sympathy as I explained that I had no claim check. How in the world would I ever get my precious big white bag with all my clothes in it? The words were hardly out of my mouth when I saw a big white bag with the words ROY ROGERS—SITMAR CRUISES on its metal tag. We grabbed it, piled into a taxi, and rushed across town to the hotel. As we approached the desk in the lobby I swallowed hard—twice —and timidly asked my fellow passenger if he could lend me five dollars until my money came. Did you ever do a thing such as that? I felt about six inches high, but he grinned and handed me a twenty-dollar bill. Then the cashier at the desk said he was sorry, but he couldn't change a bill as large as that. I swallowed hard again—three times—and his brother stepped up with a smaller bill. Now I know what it means to be humbled in the sight of strangers.

I slept very little that night, tossing and turning and telling myself that my purse would never reach me in time for my departure for DuBois, where I was to sing and speak on the last night of a crusade featuring Pat Boone, Jim Irwin, Tom Lester, and Nicky Cruz. I lay awake nursing the worry and the apprehension—and finally I turned it all over to the Lord. I simply prayed, "You know they are expecting me in DuBois, Lord, and I know You will get me there," and went to sleep.

At 8:00 A.M. there was a knock on the door, and there was a bellboy with my purse in his hand. I almost wept.

My mom said to me one day, "Frances, you need a keeper." She was right—and I've got one—the best, the Lord.

On the plane, after my initial shock had subsided, the young man and I had a real in-depth discussion about spiritual values. Just before we landed, he said, "I'm glad we met. I needed to talk to you."

I replied, "And I needed to talk to you!" I thanked him by letter when I returned the borrowed money. (I sent him a copy of *The Woman at the Well* when I got home.)

Just before I left the hotel, a beautiful thing happened. A young woman employed at the hotel asked to see me. She sat in my room and told me that a month ago she had a tremendous experience when the Holy Spirit entered her life. Suddenly her eyes were filled with tears; she said, "Mrs. Rogers,

popular "Jesus Is Just Alright." I love them. I didn't when they first appeared. Many of us used to think that these young rockers were a bit off their rockers. I've changed my mind about that. They were and are youth seeking something new, in their music. This particular group in DuBois had found something old but still new: the Gospel message. Everywhere I go I find inspired young people singing or playing "Amazing Grace" and "He's Got the Whole World in His Hands" and "I Don't Know How to Love Him," and now this "Jesus Is Just Alright." It is a sign of the times.

Flew back to Dallas, this time on United Airlines. I like that word *united.* I've just read a line about being united in Rus Walton's book *One Nation Under God:* "As Americans we must have unity, but not uniformity." I like that. Not uniformity, not all thinking and acting alike, but unity of *purpose.* Good! The Creator was wise when He made no two of us alike. What a bore that would be. He made us different so that we might all profit in the free exchange of ideas—but don't forget that He made it possible for us to be one *in spirit.*

On Wednesday I was on an early-morning news show with the lovely Roberta Hammond of WFAA-TV, CBS Dallas. We talked about my book *Let Freedom Ring,* which I had just written with Dr. Frank S. Mead. It was old home week for me, being back on WFAA, where I had worked so many years ago on an "early bird" show. It was good to rap with Roberta about our God and our country, and all through it I kept thinking of what a popular subject this has become on the air waves. Everybody seems to want to talk about it, and that's quite different from what we were thinking back in the days of wild and violent protest against everything from low wages to the Constitution. We're doing a lot more positive thinking these days.

How lucky we are to live in a country which gives us perfect freedom to broadcast our religious faith and a philosophy of life based on that faith!

From there, Bob Lossa, the very competent Revell representative, rushed me over to KPBC radio, where I talked for an hour with Zola Levitt of "The Heart of the Matter" show. One interviewer on this show referred to me as "intelligent, with plenty of smarts." It was flattering, but I'm not so smart. What intelligence I have comes out of my knowledge that God is the beginning and the end of wisdom; I take my leads from Him, and I pray daily that He will keep me humble and looking at myself objectively, that He will give me the grace to scold myself for my shortcomings and laugh at myself for my silly mistakes, and that He will keep me from taking myself too seriously.

I'm always meeting people on these trips who have read my first book, *Angel Unaware*—the story of our retarded Robin who came to lead us to a new faith. On this trip a young representative of United Airlines shared with me his experience with a retarded baby in his family. As we talked, I felt something that I always feel when I am talking with people who are going through this Gethsemane experience:

a flood of the balm of Gilead into my soul (*see* Jeremiah 8:22). To know that my little Robin continues to bless others always strengthens my appreciation of God's confidence in allowing me to mother one of His special ones, even if only for two short years.

I told this father to always, with the rest of his family, hold that baby in their hearts and to always have a special, constructive program going for her.

Many, many parents write me, asking what they should do with their retarded children, and no two cases are alike. Some families are able—and led—to take care of such children in their homes, others must—and probably should—place them in homes specially equipped to give them care and specialized education and guidance which would be impossible in the home of the parents. The French call such children "those near to the heart of God." Some may have difficulty understanding that, but I believe it with all my heart. The joy—yes, joy—of these children is pure, simple, and unfeigned. It takes little to make them happy, and it is a privilege to minister to them. I know—I have ministered and I have shared.

Fort Worth, Texas

We drove to Fort Worth this morning to tape a show with the very brilliant Bobbie Wygant (KAAS-TV, NBC). She is a big wheel in the Fort Worth—Dallas area. She asks good questions. She threw this one at me, as a starter: "You made a statement in *Let Freedom Ring* that you had no apology to offer for your country. Aren't you afraid of being challenged on a blanket statement like this, in view of Watergate and all the other corruption that is all around us today?"

I said, "To me, there is no perfect person or perfect country. There is good and bad in all of us, and good and bad in this country of ours. But in my humble opinion the good in America far outweighs the bad. I think there is no other country that tries so unselfishly to help other needy people all across the world. I make no apology for a country that tries to do that. I believe this is a great and good country— and that with the grace and help of God we can make it better."

I met another great lady in Dallas. She is a born-again Christian who came to Dallas thirty-seven years ago with $100 in her pocket and today heads a company which has sold $125-million worth of merchandise in a single year—a business which enables 15,000 women to find fulfillment and make an excellent living. Her company this year gave away $97,000 worth of groceries as a Christmas present to the home office's 310 employees; it sponsors a ranch run by loving people who minister to problem boys; and it underwrites $50,000 in scholarships to the Fellowship of Christian Athletes. Not bad at all!

Mary Crowley started all this in the conviction that if we think big enough, we can *do* it—do anything. Back in her early days, she had heard "an enormous black preacher with grizzled white hair" say, in a "booming voice as strong as a rusty tow chain, 'God doesn't take time to make a nobody,' " and she applied that to her business. Her idea was that every woman in America has the opportunity to be a *somebody,* and that she can win big if she thinks big. Of her company, Home Interiors, she says, "[We] have made it our goal to build confidence in our women. We have done it by encouraging them to put God *first* in their homes, family life, and careers." But her real reason for building this colossal enterprise was not to make a fortune for herself, but to earn money to share in a creative way—and double the enjoyment. She has more than doubled the enjoyment of problem children, cripples, and handicapped veterans. Once she told her attorney, Doug Adkins, that she wanted her will to read: "Being of sound mind I spent—and gave away—every last cent I had."

She's written a book entitled *Think Mink,* in which she tells all about it. Get that book, reader, and you'll take a trip on cloud nine. Thank you, Mary Crowley, for helping me to think big about a big God.

Lubbock, Texas

It was hot in Dallas—ninety-nine degrees in the shade, and no shade. At noon I stepped out of the plane in Lubbock—into forty-nine-degree weather and pouring rain. We rushed to the auditorium to rehearse with the Jordan Singers for a concert that night. I'm a pretty tough old trouper, but halfway through the rehearsal my legs buckled with fatigue and I almost went down. If I fail to get enough rest between engagements, and a proper food balance, I can and often do get into trouble. I was driven to the hotel where I fell on the bed for an hour, praying that God would give me the strength to get through that concert. I got up and ate a steak, and that made me feel somewhat better, but not good enough. I had my doubts about the concert, and I could just see myself going head over heels in the middle of a song.

I was far from perfect that night, but just as God's strength is made perfect in weakness, with the first song I felt the surge of energy and anticipation which comes with the realization of being used of the glory of God. Lubbock was kind and gracious to me, and gave a long standing ovation at the close of the concert. The people almost shouted their approval as they sang "The Old Rugged Cross" and the Jordan Singers' Number One hit, "Phone Call From God." I felt as though I had never been sick or exhausted.

Then there was a plus to it all when a little group of retarded children, representing the Mentally Retarded of Lubbock, presented me with a lovely rocking chair. I couldn't keep back the tears—even though I knew that Roy and I might have words over who was to sit in it, and when. I knew that the man of the house would stake a claim on it, and that there might be a verbal shoot-out over it, but that every time either he or I sat in it we would think of those beautiful people of Lubbock.

Charlotte, North Carolina

Flew into Charlotte last night, wishing I might be flying home to California, but I hadn't been in that town an hour before I was thanking God for sending me there. In Charlotte, we met the Amway people, and were they *something!* If you haven't heard about Amway, you've missed one of the great success stories of the American free-enterprise system.

It is the story of Richard DeVos and Jay Van Andel, who started a small distributing business in the basements of their homes. In 1959 they organized Amway, and moved up out of their basements to a converted gas station, and then to a small factory on a two-acre lot. Today, as I write, seventeen years later, the Amway plant covers one million square feet on a three-hundred-acre industrial spread. Charles Paul Conn, who helped DeVos write a book entitled *Believe!* (Get it!) tells us:

> Scores of products are manufactured in a fully automated plant and shipped by a fleet of fifty tractor-trailer rigs to huge warehouses located across the country. Bottles, labels, cardboard boxes, virtually everything necessary for the Amway retail operation is manufactured on the premises. A giant computer center keeps the whole operation

running smoothly. The plant's fifteen hundred employees include production workers, teams of research chemists, corporate attorneys, and data analysts. Inside the plant are new-product and quality-control laboratories, a printing plant and photo studio, and testing facilities of every description.

At the cutting edge of the company's growth is the sales force, over two hundred thousand independent Amway distributorships. Together they generate over two hundred thirty million dollars annually in estimated retail sales. In the company's history, there has never been a year when the sales graph did not climb upward. DeVos and Van Andel communicate with the distributors constantly in an endless round of sales rallies, conventions, and seminars around the country. The company offices occupy impressive quarters in the gleaming new Center of Free Enterprise, which itself attracted twenty-four thousand visitors in its first year. The company's executives crisscross the country—and travel to Amway's international operations in Canada, United Kingdom, West Germany, Australia, and Hong Kong—in a variety of vehicles that include two jet planes (with a full-time aviation crew of eight pilots and mechanics), buses, and a 116-foot yacht named, appropriately, the *Enterprise.*

The Amway Corporation is what free enterprise and the American dream are all about.

All that—in seventeen years! It *can* be done.

Now I am interested in this industrial phenomenon not only because of its startling success but also because Rich DeVos is something more than just another spectacular operator, *and because he is a man of God.* In *Believe!* he tells us what he believes in:

I believe that one of the most powerful forces in the world is the will of the man who believes in himself, who dares to aim high, to go confidently after the things that he wants from life. . . . I believe in life with a large YES and a small no. I believe that life is good, that people are good, that God is good. And I believe in affirming every day that I live, proudly and enthusiastically, that life in America under God is a positive experience! . . . The free-enterprise system is the greatest single source of our country's economic success, and its best hope for surviving the demands of this chaotic century. . . . I believe it is high time for us to get off each other's backs . . . and get on with the business of making a better life for ourselves and our children. . . . I believe in America. In a time when flag-waving is discouraged, I don't apologize at all for an old-fashioned, hand-over-heart, emotional brand of patriotism. I believe that America is the greatest country in the world, with the richest past, the brightest future, and the most exciting present of any nation anywhere.

Never before had I seen or heard such enthusiasm for this country under God. What a joy it is to realize that we still have people who appreciate the freedoms of America! Paul Conn spoke that night, just before I spoke, and he really turned me on. When I got to my feet I thought *Paul's act is a hard one to follow,* but following an overwhelming reception by the crowd, I began with: "With men such as Richard DeVos and Paul Conn and the Amway people, I am heartened for the future of our country." I meant it. These people do not sit back and whine and wonder (my apologies to President Kennedy) what their country can do for them—they roll up their sleeves and do something for their country, and what they do is beautiful. As Mary Crowley would say, they think big for a big God—and a big, God-fearing country.

Later

I'm quiet and alone, now, for an hour or so. The "tumult and the shouting" of the day is over, and I know that I need a nap. But there is something else I need more—an hour alone with Him, to rekindle my soul. So I take up His Word and I read, in Psalms 90:12, "So teach us to number our days, that we may apply our hearts unto wisdom." Thy wisdom, Lord, not mine! In The Modern Language Bible (New Berkeley Version) I found this verse translated, "Teach us so to number our days, *that we may acquire discerning minds*" (*italics mine*). Help me to sift out the wheat from the chaff, the evil from the good, the false from the true—and give me the courage to follow that which is true.

Verse 14 (KJV) reads: "O satisfy us early with thy mercy; that we may rejoice and be glad all our days." That humbles me. Your mercy to me has been as wide and as deep as the seven seas. It isn't enough for me just to say "Thank You." Help me to live my thanks.

Verse 15 continues: "Make us glad according to the days wherein thou hast afflicted us, and the years wherein we have seen evil." Evil—or calamity. Thank You, Father, for the afflictions You have sent my way. They have taught me so much. They have lifted me out of an empty living into a life that is glorious, and I am grateful, as I have learned of Thy purpose.

Verse 16 tells us: "Let thy work appear unto thy servants, and thy glory unto their children." Or, "*Reveal* thy work. . . ." I have had many revelations of Thy work and power in my life: keep my mind and heart and soul open to those I know will come, tomorrow and tomorrow and tomorrow.

Thank You for listening, Lord—and for speaking to me.

Later Still

I needed that moment of quietness with God; shortly after I had said, "Amen," and spent a few moments wondering about the meaning of acquiring a discerning mind, I picked up a newspaper and read the awful story of a man and a woman who seemed to have no minds at all—or who had evil minds, at best. They had burned and beaten their child to death. I read in this account that child abuse is the number-one killer in the state of Florida, according to a report on the subject by International Orphans, Incorporated—of which our daughter Cheryl is an active member. She tells me that the average child abuser is a middle-class college graduate. It blew my mind, and made my heart tremble.

What are we teaching or not teaching in our schools and colleges that makes a woman incapable of handling frustration to the point of child abuse? That goes for a man, too, for quite often a man is involved with the woman. As a matter of fact, that is most often the case. What does this say to us? Does it mean that we have become so affluent that we are satiated with things, and decadent, feeling that we are on a treadmill of spiritual drought, and flailing out at innocent children in our anger? Are we listening too much to the siren voice of "Do your own thing, express yourself, find yourself, no matter who is hurt as you do it"? Can it be that these degenerate men and woman are sick with meaninglessness, that they are unable to discern good from evil? I'll be praying over this in the days ahead.

That's all for today. I must pack for another plane ride, another chance to witness.

Tempe, Arizona

Here I sit, looking out of my hotel window at this beautiful Arizona landscape. In a few moments I will be on my way to speak at the Grace Community Church Fiesta of Faith. And believe it or not, I'm staying at the Fiesta Hotel.

Fiesta! What a happy word to hook up with faith! *Fiesta*, as you probably know, comes from an old Spanish word meaning "feast," and Christianity is a constant feast or celebration of our faith in God, His Christ, and His Holy Spirit.

But sometimes we stumble over circumstances that make it hard for us to be happy. This lovely spot in the Arizona desert is a spiritual oasis for me, for I came here carrying a heavy burden for one of my children. Most mothers have a habit of going all-out for the children they love; we pray, and when God's help does not come quickly, we step in and try to carry the burden alone. This is one of the worst weaknesses, and sometimes it "bugs" me to no end, for I know I shouldn't do it.

Yesterday and last night I could hardly pray. Old Satan had thrown one of his smoke screens around me, and I was both miserable and bewildered—which is just what the devil wanted. There didn't seem to be any way out of it, and in desperation I asked God to help me: "Lift me out of this; I'm so *paralyzed.*" Then I fell asleep, and as I slept, He lifted.

When I went down to breakfast, there was His matchless Arizona sun bathing me in its warm glow, and penetrating the gloom of my frustrated thinking. I bowed my head and thanked Him for it, and His joy filled my soul; I began to rejoice in the Spirit. God was in His heaven, and all was right in my world. I broke through the smoke screen and walked in the blessed light of His love and wisdom. I knew then that my function is not to impatiently try to nudge God into action but to love and wait upon Him.

I know—some of you readers will wonder about all of this; you will be thinking that because I have been used of God in writing books on Christian faith and in speaking up for Him on the road that the answers must come easy to me, and that my life is all smooth sailing. No, it isn't that way at all. Behind the scenes, "offstage," back where you can't see them, there are temptations, snares, obstacles, headaches, and heartaches. It seems to become harder and harder as life goes on, and as Satan's obstacles become higher and higher. But I have discovered this: *God always gives me extra strength to get over them.*

Whenever I get caught in one of these worry fits, I take up God's Fiesta Book and read the story of David fighting his desperate battles against the Philistines. There were many times when the battle seemed hopeless, when David was tempted to quit and go home—but always, *always,* the driving strength of the Almighty poured down upon him, and he fought on. At one moment, after Saul and Jonathan had been slain and there seemed to be no hope, David tells us, "The sorrows of hell compassed me about; the snares of death prevented [enveloped] me" (2 Samuel 22:6), and he turned to God and "He delivered me . . . . by my God have I leaped over a wall" (verses 18, 30). Over the wall of Satan's obstacles, over the wall that to human eyes seemed insurmountable but over which any man can leap, with the lifting power of God! That isn't just a sentimental, comforting *idea:* it has been my *experience.*

Yes, there are times when Satan whispers to me, "Why don't you give up? Can't you see that all these troubles of yours are just payment for the years when you listened to me instead of listening to God? God didn't like that. He is still punishing you for your past waywardness. Praying won't help you, and God isn't going to bless you. Why don't you just quit?" Satan is no fool; his timing is good; he waits until you are in deep trouble, and then he lets you have it. He *seems* to make sense in moments when your heart and mind are torn and desperate for help, but he is a gigantic liar, and his words are nonsense to any Christian who knows that "greater is he [God] that is in you, than he that is in the world" (1 John 4:4).

There are two ways out of any difficulty, two ways in which to get over Satan's wall: one is to boot Satan out of your thinking and put your mind on God; the other is to go out and help someone with burdens greater than your own.

I've learned how to clobber the devil—the disappointments and the frustrations and the worries. I have learned how to say, "Go chase yourself, Satan. I've got a big fat flash for you: You will never destroy my faith or my witness to the grace and saving power of God in Christ and His Holy Spirit; you can never build a wall that is too high for *us* to get over. Do your worst; God will outdo you."

Satan's strategy is good; I despise him, but I must admit that he's good at his job. He picks the most vulnerable spots in our armor. With a woman, that spot is usually her love for her children. No matter how old or young that child may be, she still feels the old maternal instinct to protect, which prompts her to step in and fend off whatever it is that brings trouble to the child. We mothers love our children, even when they are fifty years old, and we want them around us forever. When they "fly the coop," when the last child leaves home and goes out on his own—that is a bad day for Mother! It seems as though they no longer need or want her.

She's wrong about that, in most cases, but many mothers still believe it, and they refuse to let go. They cling to the idea that they are *still* responsible for their children. They (and I, too,) are mothers who need to read the old Chinese proverb that says, "When the tree is grown, the branches are spread."

How come we mothers can't be like the eagle—the mother eagle who, when her children are ready to fly, pushes them out of the nest? If they flounder around in the air and start a long dive to death on the ground, she flies under them and takes them back to the nest. If they haven't the courage to try it again, she makes the nest so rough and uncomfortable that they just have to get out of there. They either "fly right" or they do not survive.

Your children may have more survival power than you think.

Of course, I'm no eagle. I am just a mother who loves her children and wants to help them—but God saves me from putting myself between the children and His way of teaching them to "fly" on their own.

So, on this bright, sunny morning, I think of Jesus saying, ". . . he that loveth son or daughter more than me is not worthy of me" (Matthew 10:37). And I have the answer. Lord, please stay with me and help me to keep my priorities straight.

Home

One reads about hijackings, kidnappings, murders, tear gas, and bombs, but probably nine out of every ten of us tends to think, *Too bad—but it would never happen to* me. I was like that—until last night, when I was teargassed and bombed.

Roy and I had gone to Beverly Hills for the premiere showing of Corrie ten Boom's incredible story *The Hiding Place.* I had seen the film previously, at a private showing at the Christian Booksellers' Convention in Anaheim in July, but I wanted Roy to see it. Frankly, I wanted to see it again, for its message was powerful and its witness was overwhelming. In case you haven't seen it, or read the book, this is the story of heroic Corrie ten Boom, who stood her ground for

Christ under fierce persecution by the Nazis during World War II. She even had it in her heart to forgive the concentration-camp Nazi who would have killed her. If that isn't faith in action, tell me what it is.

So we went to the premiere—along with a huge crowd which included a lot of film and television personalities, ministers, priests, and rabbis. Billy Graham was there; it was his film company that had produced the film. We talked with Billy for a while before entering the theater. The first time I saw *The Hiding Place* I couldn't help being thrilled at the courage of Billy and his co-workers in making this movie— and I couldn't help wondering whether they would be 100 percent true to Corrie's account of her imprisonment with her sister, Betsie. They were true to it, thank God.

We chatted briefly with Corrie, who stood so tall and faithful that the sight of her filled my old eyes with tears, and with Jeanette Clift, a wonderful actress who played the part of Corrie in the movie. I looked around at this collection of so many greats in show business, and thanked God again.

We found seats in the middle section of the theater and relaxed—but not for long. Suddenly, there was a short, muffled report—it sounded like a pistol with a silencer—off to the right front. Several people near the explosion leaped to their feet, cupped their hands over their faces, and ran for the center aisle, waving to the rest of us to get out. By the time Roy and I reached the lobby we were choking and holding our hands over our burning eyes. Tear gas!

Pat Boone, an excellent master of ceremonies and an old

trouper for Christ, stayed in his place on stage, talking, and was one of the last to come out. We stood in the street, waiting for the police to clear the gas from the theater. I was getting madder by the minute. What kind of degenerate could do a thing such as this? He should get life imprisonment! Then I saw Corrie walking through the crowd, beaming, laughing, delighting them with her sincerity and her great sense of humor. What a Christian she is. It never seemed to occur to her to hate those who had placed the bomb.

Few people left. For an hour we stood there in the street, singing gospel songs and Israeli songs. What a happening, *in Beverly Hills.* We didn't go until the police told us that it would be impossible to show the film that night because the gas had settled in the carpeting.

Then we left there and went to the Beverly Hills Hotel, where Billy Graham and Corrie reminded us that "All things work together for good to them that love God . . ." (Romans 8:28), and that the swastika-banded bomb was actually a blessing in disguise. This would give terrific publicity to the movie all over the country, drawing people who otherwise might not see it, thinking it was just another religious film. It did just that. Thank You, Lord.

I had a long talk that night with Jeanette Clift, who played the lead role in the movie. She told me that she had heard my witness years ago, when Roy and I were appearing in Houston at the Fat Stock and Rodeo Show, and that it had so discomfited her in her determination to become a star actress that she finally said yes to the Lord in total commitment of her life. She said, with a lovely laugh, "You irritated me to no end, and I was pretty angry about it, especially when you said that being a Christian was the greatest thing in your life and that show business paled in comparison. At the time, I was deeply involved in studying dramatics, and I was driven by an intense ambition to reach the top in show biz, at any cost, but that witness of yours turned me around and now I am intensely interested in doing what God wants me to do."

Since *The Hiding Place* was being shown, she said, she had been receiving many tempting and attractive offers to work in other movies—but she asks the Lord in prayer to help her make decisions about them. I sat there, speechless, for a while; I hadn't known anything about all of this, hadn't known that my Gospel seed had fallen upon such good ground. I could only thank a God who works in mysterious ways, His wonders to perform.

We never know what influence we have for good or bad, in action or the spoken word—and it comes as a spiritual bonus when someone tells us that we have had an influence in some crucial moment of their lives. What a responsibility we have, as Christians. Sometimes, when our haloes begin to slip or tighten, it is well to remember that people are watching and listening and wondering what we are going to do about it. Haloes bother me just as it bothers me when people think of me as "good." I am not good at all. Christ is good and if there is any one thing that even smacks of goodness about *me,* it is His Spirit working through me. As Paul put it, "For I know that in me (that is, in my flesh,) dwelleth no good thing" (Romans 7:18).

It is the Spirit that quickens the Christian into action, as he yields to the Lord. That's a truth that has been worked out in my life. Some folks think because I have been given the privilege of sharing my life in witnessing before mass audiences, or in sharing my faith in writing my books, that I have all the answers to any problem that besets me, before the problem appears. That isn't so, at all. I haven't any answers—but God has. By loving Him, trusting in Him, and studying His Word, direction and understanding come in His own time and in His own way. The Lord's house is not a mail-order house where you place an order for an article of certain size, description, and price to be delivered on a certain date. But God knows what we want, and more important, what it is good for us to have. He knows all about our tendency to "order" something, before we call, and He answers us as He thinks best. Sometimes the package we get is surprisingly different from what we had in mind. The cost may be considerably higher than we planned to pay, or sometimes the package is larger than we expected, and the price is less. He knows best what to send, and when. Sometimes we ask amiss, and do not receive at all, and we complain about that.

There is an old saying which goes, "Be careful what you ask in prayer, for you just might get it."

Louisville, Kentucky

I am lying on a heating pad, propped up on pillows in my room at the Galt House. I came here for a Sunday-school Emphasis program for the Church of the Nazarene and had some bad bumps along the way. The Lord had to help me to get on my feet for the speech this morning.

Yesterday, in Memphis, I wrenched my back getting myself and my mom into the backseat of my uncle's car. That was bad enough, but to compound the misery I thought I had lost a lovely bracelet watch which Roy had given me one Mother's Day—a big dial watch that I could see and read without my glasses. I muttered and wept, and crawled all over the floor on all fours, wondering what I would tell Roy. Finally I just gave up. I said, "Lord, You know how my back hurts and You know where that watch is. If I really need the watch, I know You will lead me to it. Amen." Later, while I was hanging my sweater jacket in the closet, it tumbled out of the cuff! I thanked Him, got some sleep, and then did pretty well with the speech.

My young friend of many years, Judy Whisenant, said to me the other day over the phone, "Please take care of yourself; you are always doing for others; how about stopping long enough once in a while to do something for Dale Evans?" I could only say to her what I have so often said to

Mom: "Unto whomsoever much is given, of him shall be much required" (Luke 12:48).

That reminds me of something dear Dr. Louis Evans, Sr. said the last time he visited our home: "I pray that when I am no longer of value to the Lord in preaching and teaching, He will stop the invitations from coming." It seems as though Dr. Evans, like Dale Evans, wants to go "with his boots on." He has a chronic illness, and though his face and his hands may tremble, the voice rings clear and true with Christian conviction. Thank You, Lord, for sending him our way.

En Route to Vancouver, Canada

We are more than halfway to Vancouver, where I am to speak at a women's rally, and I've got to settle down, pretty quickly, and outline my music for tonight. But right now, some thousands of feet in the air, I'm wishing we could just stay up here forever, and enjoy it.

I'm getting a Lord's-eye view of some of the most colorful real estate in the world. The scene outside my window is breathtaking. The sky is a riot of color—mauve, pink, white, several shades of blue. Down below us I see a range of magnificent mountains, black and brown, and great, wide areas of blocks of green at their feet. What a gigantic palette of colors God used to paint this world. My heart sings with the song of Ecclesiastes 3:11: "He hath made every thing beautiful in his time." And I remember those lines from Elizabeth Barrett Browning, which I have jotted down in my notebook:

> Earth's crammed with heaven
> And every common bush afire with God;
> But only he who sees, takes off his shoes. . . .

That's it. Nature is no accidental creation; it is the handiwork of God, and it praises Him with ten thousand voices.

And I call to mind the words of Walt Whitman, telling us of how he once went to hear a learned astronomer lecture. He became confused with the battalion of charts, diagrams, proofs, and figures, and at last:

> . . . I became tired and sick;
> Till rising and gliding out, I wander'd off by myself.
> In the mystical moist night-air, and . . .
> Look'd up in perfect silence at the stars.

You were no churchman, old Walt, but here you were surely praising God. Thank you.

Color! My friend Joy Eilers wrote a song that I often sing in public and privately; it is called "What Color Is Love?" and her last line is: "The hues of the rainbow were fashioned by One / Who's the very same color,/ Just the same color as love." And so it is. The color of God is love. He is all color, all in all. I feel certain, up here looking at His splashing of color in nature, that all that He has made is filled with His glory and beauty, that all of it is part of His plan and purpose. How can any of us look at it, and not take off his shoes? This is, as Moses said, holy ground (*see* Exodus 3:5).

His love is not confined to nature, much as I love it there; I have found it in my relations with people. Last night, for instance, was my son Tom's birthday. With his family, I went to a birthday party at the famous Pepe's Restaurant in Burbank and we had a wonderful time. My first great-grandchild was there—little Amy Elizabeth, age one. Thank You for her, Lord, and for the love I see gleaming in her eyes, and for the love that ran around that table among all of us. Thank You for my children, my grandchildren, and now (I can't believe it) my great-grandchildren. There is another grandchild on the way—and another great-grandchild. Candi and Todd Halberg (Tom's middle girl) are expecting a child in May. Candi is a diabetic. Please watch over her, Lord, and over that child. Tom's youngest, Julie, will graduate from high school next May. How richly I am blessed, with this brood to love as they love me.

A thought just occurred to me, as I sat here thinking of those young people: There may be some young ones in the audience I face tonight who will feel no need of Jesus Christ in their lives—such as the young man who said to me a while back, "You have no right to try to convert people to *your* way." He didn't realize that I cannot convert anybody—not

I alone. The Holy Spirit must convict all of us of our lack and need—all I can do is to give the reasons for the faith that is within *me,* as my Bible tells me to. The rest is something between the needy and their God.

That young man may not feel the need now, but one day he will, as sure as God made little green apples. How sad it is to see others such as him who, driven to the wall by the vicissitudes of life, have no spiritual resources with which to cope. This fellow said he was an agnostic, but somehow I think he knew he was a man in need of God. He has my prayers, until the Lord tells me to stop praying for him. I was privileged to be able to plant a seed of faith in him; God will water it, later, and there will be a great rejoicing over one sinner who has repented. If God wants that to happen, it will happen. I am content to leave it with Him.

With my own children, I have been privileged to sow the same seed of faith, and I have tried diligently to train them up "in the way they should go" (*see* Proverbs 22:6). If they depart from The Way, as I did in my youth, then they, too, will be welcomed home by the Father when they come to Him in the end, of themselves, and they will be instructed in the ways of righteousness in such a way that they will lose their taste for that which is harmful and not pleasing to the Father. I know so well how hard those lessons are to learn, but He will see that they learn, and He will never fail them, if they love Him and trust Him. As Walter Cronkite says as he signs off, "And that's the way it is. . . ."

Home

Everything went well in Vancouver. The crowd of women in the meeting at the Bayshore Inn was warm in welcoming and praying with me. And while I didn't know it, I had need of a warm heart to face what was coming the next day.

This was on Saturday night. I was to catch a plane at noon on Sunday. At 2:45 A.M. on Sunday, I was nearly tumbled out of my bed, which shook and rocked as though all the imps of hell were shaking it. I got out of that bed in one second flat; being a Californian, I knew it was either an earth tremor or a downright earthquake. Half-awake, I stood there wondering if a tidal wave could reach my room on the seventh floor of the hotel. But it all quieted down as suddenly as it came, and I thanked God, stumbled back into bed, and slept until 9:30 A.M., when I got up and looked out of the window at a raging snowstorm! First an earthquake, and now a blizzard. It was a bit much, even for this old "What else is new?" trail traveler. What next?

I attended church via TV while I packed, had a quick breakfast, and asked the bell captain in the lobby if he would get a cab for me. He smiled sadly; he could guarantee nothing —but there was a couple who were set to leave in a cab in ten minutes, and if I could make it, I could go with them. I made it, don't ask me how, and off we went into the wild, white yonder, loaded down with baggage. That cab must have weighed fifty tons, at least.

We climbed a high hill and came to a squealing stop when a traffic light hidden over the top of the hill suddenly turned red. The driver jammed on his brakes and we skidded into a snowbank. It took three men to push us out. Three blocks later we had a flat tire—no spare, no snowplows, people stuck everywhere. It looked like the end—until the cab company sent out another cab. The new driver was either afraid of bogging down or he wanted to give us a thrill, for he pushed his accelerator down to the floor and we went zigzagging and jackknifing from one side of the street to the other, barely missing cars stuck in the snow on both sides of us. I covered my face with my hands and moaned, "Oh, to die this way in Vancouver!" I hadn't had a ride such as this since 1972 during my visit to Rome, where there are no speed limits for automobiles—and where every driver knows it and steps on the gas as though speed were going out of style.

But we made it to the airport—only to discover that our plane, too, was stuck somewhere in the snow and that there would be quite a delay. Thank heaven, I had a day free before witnessing at a mass meeting in Everett, Washington, with the Kroese Brothers, so I wasn't worried very much. The plane finally arrived and we took off; we reached Seattle about 8:00 P.M. I "hit the hay," bedded down thankful for being alive and for being back in the United States and for a few hours of badly needed rest.

I've heard a lot of people complain about life in hotel rooms—but I've come to love them as havens of rest, where one can wait upon the Lord in blessed silence. There is so much to be done, when I am at home; the phone rings constantly and people are coming and going, and I find it almost impossible to quiet myself long enough to communicate with my Lord. There's an old saying, "The road to hell is paved with good intentions," and I believe it. We plan to do this or that *right away*—and then the phone rings, and we forget what it was we were going to do. The living room needs cleaning—so we forget that moment of prayer that means so much. Our good intentions get blocked off by the most unexpected happenings, and the intention never gets transformed into action. It's maddening.

Forgive me, Lord, for letting it become maddening. Forgive me when I fail to follow Your directives, whether because of fatigue or carelessness or an uncentered, wandering mind. Sometimes, Lord, my mind is filled to overflowing with all sorts of ideas and responsibilities, and they writhe around in my poor head like the arms of an octopus. At such a time I need You to help me slow down and get things straightened out. I need to go out of the house, stand still, breathe deeply and slowly, and say, "Take over, Lord; center me down on what You want me to do."

Back at the ranch, we shared the Thanksgiving feast with Cheryl, Marion, Dodie, Dusty, and respective families. The children prepared and brought the food, and I filled in what they didn't bring. We always do that at our family gatherings because, traveling as I do, I just can't shoulder the whole load. We make Thanksgiving a day of sharing. I travel so much, since the children "flew the coop" and went off to establish their own homes and families, that I just can't do a lot of things for my husband, my mom, my desk, and my house that I would like to do. Often I hate to leave them for another witnessing trip. Often I want to stay home and cook. Some of my cooking experiments turn out well, and some don't. Oh, well, you can't win 'em all.

Which reminds me—Christmas is just around the corner. We used to have great family get-togethers at Christmas, before the children's families got so big and kept getting bigger. Nowadays, we feel that Christmas Day is a day for *each* family, and that they are entitled to celebrate the day in their own homes. We no longer expect our children to make the long trip to Apple Valley. We try to visit them sometime before Christmas. We like that better—especially when we remember the exhausting noise and hassles of the children, and the frantic effort to organize a dinner for twenty-eight to thirty-five youngsters and their parents. Even with help in the kitchen, I would be done in by 9:00 P.M. if I tried it at my age!

I'm getting a few days rest now—and a chance to fill in the diary with some odds and ends that seem important.

Not long ago I was checking my jewelry, and I found my favorite cross with its pendant chain all tangled up with a pair of crystal earrings. I hadn't been wearing the cross on my television shows because I felt that it didn't look good with the earrings. Now it was hopelessly snarled up, and it took me a long time to disengage it; I was afraid that I would have to break the chain to get it loose. I fussed and I fumed, and suddenly I was filled with shame for failing to wear the cross as evidence of my faith. When it finally came free and I clasped it around my neck, I vowed that never again would I take it off for fashion's sake. My cheeks burned as I thought to myself, "Nobody *asked* me to take it off." It won't happen again.

At around the same time, I mislaid my single strand of cultured pearls, a gift from Roy just after the birth of little Robin. I hoped to find them somewhere in my luggage, for pearls have a really spiritual significance for me. Faith in Christ represents the pearl of great price (*see* Matthew 13:-46), and so the pearl is my favorite gem. But—no, they were nowhere to be found. I'd lost them, and it was likely that someone else had found them.

Whoever found them and still has them has my prayer that he or she will find the Pearl of Great Price in Jesus Christ.

I forgot to record an interview I had on my last trip, with a radio man. He was good: he led me into a discussion of democracy; the falling apart of our morals; our disregard of the Constitution; and the erosion of patriotism and of the biblical principles on which our nation is grounded. Inevitably, we got around to the scriptural idea that any house will collapse unless it is built on the foundation rock of faith in God (*see* Matthew 7:24–27). It was an inspiring interview, and I have been thinking about that house ever since.

Early morning planning in my kitchen at home. *Below:* Then some play time in the backyard with Max, our German Shepherd watchdog.

At the Church of the Valley with Pastor O. William Hansen. *Below:* Time to check music and rehearse for out-of-town engagement.

Jotting down some notes on the manuscript for this book in my office. *Below:* Now to the type-writer to get it all down!

This grandfather clock is one of my prize possessions—Roy gave it to me the first year of our marriage. *Below:* The plants need attention too.

Time out for a quick bite at the kitchen counter. *Below:* This wonderful rocker was presented to me in Lubbock, Texas.

Packing clothes for my next trip —this is in the dressing room. *Below:* My office is a quiet, comfortable place to study the Bible.

On my way to Ontario, California, airport—first, lock the front door. *Below:* Have to make a quick stop at the Roy Rogers, Dale Evans Museum in Victorville, California.

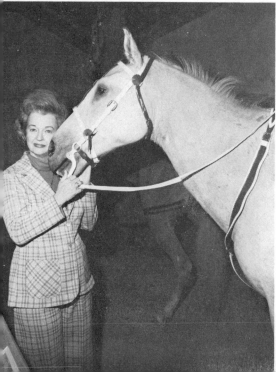

Inside the museum—here's my book and record album display. *Left:* And of course, here's Buttermilk, also at the museum.

Check-in time at Ontario, California, airport. *Right:* I do have ten minutes for coffee at the airport lunch counter.

Boarding time. *Right:*I settle
down for a pleasant trip.

I got some new slants on the house.

I believe that *any* house not built of cement or on a rock can burn—*but the foundation will not burn.* And a life that is almost burned out in sin can be reconstructed—if the foundation is God-based.

There is nothing wrong with our national foundation or with our Constitution. What is wrong is our refusal to abide by the Constitution, individually and collectively. It will work, if we have the courage to do what it suggests. Yes, dishonesty, greed, sloth, immorality, the lust for power, and a crass materialism have spread a rotten film over the luster of the beautiful and possible American dream. All manner of Americans—businessmen, lawyers, congressmen, doctors —have smeared it. I think a lot about the doctors, for our lives are so often in their hands, and I tremble at the thought of the *corrupt* physician. But it isn't so much the doctors who are corrupt as it is the awful rip-off of malpractice suits brought against them by patients and lawyers who will do anything for a buck. Granted, there are often valid reasons for a malpractice suit—when negligence can be proved, or when unnecessary surgery is performed for a high fee. But these, I believe, are exceptional and not universal. I believe that most doctors are playing the game by a better set of rules.

What really gets me down is the current corruption of our faith in God.

Just a little while ago I read a magazine article which informed me that in the Soviet Union, sex and violence are not permitted on the screen. That seemed good at first, but as I thought it over I came to the conclusion that it was ironic that while the Russian government has put a ban on pornography, it does not believe in God, while in the United States we believe in God but allow our younger generation to morally strangle in a flood of X-rated films and books. How come?

The author of this magazine article said that he stood in line at the Kremlin for several hours, waiting to view the remains of the great Lenin. He called Lenin "the Russian God." And he commented after he had seen the body (there is some feeling that it may not be Lenin's body but only a wax figure), "God wore a baggy suit."

Now it is my conviction that something such as that is happening to us in the United States. Before we laugh at the poor, deluded Russians who attempt to make a God of their Lenin, suppose we take a good look at ourselves. In the United States we are mostly a people who acknowledge the existence of a supreme, Almighty God. But in our flagrant misuse of freedom as license, we are too often trying to reshape the Creator into the form of the creature. In other words, many of us are saying, in deeds if not in words, the very thing that the atheist says—that man is God. May God have mercy upon us and help us to look up to Him and not down to man as our criterion for perfection!

It is a shattering thought, but we'd better think it through before it is too late.

A young man asked me recently, "In the face of Watergate

and all this other corruption, what do you have to say to a young person who is groping for real direction in his life?" I told him that I think we have to start with ourselves, to find out how corrupt we may be in our own individual spheres of activity. We have to sweep our own doorsteps clean before we grumble about our neighbor's doorstep. Then I would advise the young to read the Bible, praying to God to unlock its meaning and make it applicable to their lives. Let them read and digest the commandments of God, the words of the prophets, and the teachings of Jesus and His supreme sacrifice on Calvary in atonement for our sins and failures. Let them read it one section after another, in sequence, and they will find themselves equipped to face the all-important decisions of their lives.

Then they will definitely be on their way to complete fulfillment of their potential as human beings—plus being groomed for life everlasting.

All this was obviously a bit hard for the young man to understand, for he said, "I know—but some people do not see it just the way you do; many people, *religious* people, come to God by another way. Some believe simply in a Supreme Being, but they can't accept the whole package of Christian theology, as you do. Would you call them insincere, and turn your back on them? And what about the sincere agnostics and atheists? Isn't an honest agnostic more to be admired than a hypocritical Christian?"

I said to that, "No, I wouldn't turn my back on them, any more than Jesus would. Yes, we all need to study and examine and check every item in our theologies; they make a bewildering package, at times, and we must constantly check them out, sort the wheat from the chaff, the true from the false. That's why I pray constantly. But tell me—*don't you think the young agnostic and the young atheist need direction, too?*" I quoted John 1:9 to remind him that there is one true Light, or guidance, "which lighteth every man that cometh into the world," and I suggested that it is up to the agnostic or nonbeliever, if he is really honest and sincere in his search, to at least consider that Light. If he seeks thus, he shall find; if he knocks, the door will be opened (*see* Luke 11:9).

Johnny Cash has a great song—a best-seller among his records for a long time—entitled "I Walk the Line." Johnny walks the line that leads him to Christ. Such walking, to me, is like walking a tightrope. Have you noticed that the tightrope walker in a circus keeps his eyes on his destination—which is the platform at the other end of the rope? If he should look down at his feet, or at the ground way down there beneath him, he is likely to become overbalanced and take a fatal dive to the ground. And do you remember Peter, who was told to get out of the boat and walk on the water on that dangerous, unpredictable Sea of Galilee? Peter started out all right—in deep faith in Jesus. "But when he saw the wind boisterous," he suddenly became afraid, and started to sink (Matthew 14:30). Just for a moment, he took his eyes and his heart from Jesus, gave way to fear, and that did it!

I often think of those runaway slaves in the old South, before the Civil War began. They were illiterate; they couldn't read words, and what was worse for runaways, they couldn't read a map. A runaway had to travel a long and dangerous road all the way to Canada, mostly at night. But that slave knew one thing, and he knew it well. He knew that up there in the night sky there was a star that didn't move around as the rest of the stars did. It was the North Star, and he knew that if he kept his eyes on that star, as he floundered through dismal swamps and along unknown rivers and highways, he would make it to Canada and freedom. But let him take his eye off that star, lose it among all the other stars, and he would be hopelessly lost, and would quite likely be recaptured and returned to his master.

The Lord, he firmly believed, hung that star out to guide him. And the Lord comes to us to show us The Way. If we follow Him, we stop being lost.

It has happened to me, whenever I have taken the eyes of my mind and soul off Jesus to look to people and the world for guidance. In many a rough situation, I have felt myself sinking spiritually; the peace and the sense of direction was gone, and chaos was taking over—and then when I got my eyes on Him again, it all became clear!

I am told by my Bible to pray unceasingly (*see* 1 Thessalonians 5:17). I am also told in Ephesians 5:20 to *always* give thanks unto God, in *all* circumstances, good or bad. That's a tall order. I often find it hard to obey. It is desperately difficult to give thanks in the hard, hurtful places of life, but I have learned to do it, and if I can learn to do it, anyone can.

It is hard for me today, when I see my mother so sick that she is unable to hold down a sip of water, so weak she can barely raise her arms, unable to feed herself without panting from exhaustion. It is difficult for me to see her so, for she has been such a terrific influence in my life. I owe the dedication of my son Tom to her influence in his early years. Something in me rebels when I hear her say that she wants to be with the Lord if she can never walk again—and then I get on my knees and thank God for her, and for giving me such a mother. Then peace comes.

Through my tears I have thanked God for the privilege of ministering to our retarded angel unaware, little Robin; for her life, for her passing, for what *she* taught *me.* I thank God for sending our little adopted Korean daughter, Debbie, whom He took home from a church bus. I thank Him for taking our son Sandy home after a fatal accident in Germany. Debbie and Sandy both asked Jesus to save them for eternity at a Billy Graham Youth Night in the Los Angeles Coliseum.

I find myself saying, "Thank You, Jesus; I don't quite understand all these sorrows, but I know they have led me to a closer walk with Thee." In the years following all these tragedies, God has shown me great good coming out of them all. Had I stiffened my neck in resistance to His will, I would have been crushed by them.

"In all things give thanks" (*see* Ephesians 5:20). This is the overcoming factor in a committed Christian's life. As Benjamin Franklin said when the delegates to the Constitutional Convention had argued themselves into a hopeless impasse and the fate of the new republic dangled in the balance while they argued:

> I have lived, Sir, a long time, and the longer I live, the more convincing proofs I see of this truth—*that God governs in the affairs of men.* And if a sparrow cannot fall to the ground without his notice, is it probable that an empire can rise without his aid?

Right, Ben Franklin! God does indeed have the last word. Since He created all, He *should* have the last word, for He knows all. Imagine the audacity of those pusillanimous minds of ours to think we do not need God! Bow your heads, Americans, and thank Him for your country. Bow your heads and your knees and most of all, your hearts to the One who has lifted us to freedom, lest you sink down in the muck and mire of deadly decadence—into the oblivion which has come to the power-drunk civilizations which have preceded ours.

Later

I'm mad. Roy was recently interviewed by a young free-lance writer, and I can't believe what that writer has said about my husband in a widely circulated magazine. He quoted Roy as using profane vocabulary in his stand against filth in the films. It was horrible—and totally untrue. In all the years I have known Roy, I have never heard him use this sort of vulgar, blasphemous language in an interview.

At first I wanted Roy to sue him, but when I cooled down I realized that a lawsuit would only give the article more publicity. In some ways, the article was accurate and well done, but toward the end it seems as though the writer felt he had to insert something of shock content, to go along with the "tell it as it is" trend—dirty words and all. It's the same as a cow giving a good can of rich milk and then putting her foot in it. I'm no prude; I know all the words. I've been around a long time, and I have seen a lot of good people ruined by such writing. My blood pressure really jumps when I find someone defaming the character of a good man who for years on end has had the confidence and admiration of young and old alike—this, in my book, is a pretty shabby business.

Somehow, I feel sorry that such a good writer has to stoop so low to attract attention. It is a hard thing to bear. Help me to bear it, Lord.

Later Still

Halfway between Los Angeles and Apple Valley, on my way home from Vancouver via Seattle, I called Roy to tell him that I was on my way. He said, "Hurry, Dale; Mom is in the hospital. She has suffered a cardiac attack and she's in intensive care; the doctors have decided to insert a pacemaker." Somehow, I got through an autographing party at the Apple Valley Bible Book store the next morning, and rushed to the hospital with Roy and our pastor, Bill Hansen, to be with Mom during the operation. They were unable to give her an anesthetic, and could only deaden the area where the incision was made.

The waiting was something more than difficult. We prayed together, in the waiting room, thanking God for His presence with us. I sat there thinking back to the days when I was young—young and thinking that I could *never* lose my mother. Whenever that crossed my mind, I would try to push it away. But now I lived with the knowledge that she was in God's hands, and that He would take her home to a land where there is no illness or pain, but only peace. Jesus promised us that. Blessed promise! Without this assurance, I couldn't have lived through those torturing hours in the hospital.

When the time comes for her to leave this vale of tears, He will give us grace and comfort to bear it; He will hold us and here in His everlasting arms.

Mom made it. It was not time, yet, for her to go.

We celebrated Christmas with her—the first Christmas I had ever spent in a hospital room. How thankful I was to be able to be with her on that day.

Tulsa, Oklahoma

I left Mom in a nursing home for a trip to Tulsa, Oklahoma, and I'm worried about her lack of improvement. To top that, I had to leave Roy, who came down with pneumonia two weeks ago. He's snapping back, but still doesn't feel just right, and I felt a bit guilty, leaving him for Tulsa. Only the Spirit of my risen Christ could have given me the strength to go—and He did, and here I am, with the sun bright outside my window in the plane, and His light bright in my heart.

I say "He" and "His" and not "She," as some of my good women's libber friends think I should. What a lot of nonsense this is! To me, God is God, and the gender doesn't worry me one little bit. God is a very big God—bigger than we mere mortals can comprehend—wiser, kinder, more merciful and forgiving than we could ever be, whether we are men or women. The fact that God loves *me,* one little individual among all the trillions of people He has created, boggles my mind, but I believe it. I *know* it.

> For I am persuaded, that neither death, nor life, nor angels, nor principalities, nor powers, nor things present, nor things to come, Nor height, nor depth, nor any other creature, shall be able to separate us from the love of God, which is in Christ Jesus our Lord.
>
> Romans 8:38,39

That's enough for me.

In Tulsa, I visited with Oral Roberts. Have you met him? You *must!* Have you ever seen his fabulous Oral Roberts University? Man alive, it's something! I marvel at this man who built this amazing institution.

Oral doesn't take credit for building it; he gives all the glory and credit to God who sent His Spirit to work through Oral Roberts. Oral thinks big for God, and God does big things through him.

His idea of "seed faith" (Write him about that!) has sprouted and blossomed in nobody knows how many human hearts. He has given his whole life to this work for God, but I have heard him say, many times, "You can't outgive God."

He's right about that. All we are, all our strengths, love, and talent, come from God. That makes Him and us receivers of a bounty beyond price. But Oral believes that as stewards entrusted with such riches we shall be called into account for our stewardship, which includes our time as well as our money. One day God will ask us, "What did you do with it?"

Tampa, Florida

Roy still isn't feeling up to par since his bout with pneumonia. His movie *McIntosh and T.J.* was being premiered at Lubbock, Texas, and I had to go in his place, two days ahead of the premiere, to talk with the press. When that was over,

I had to fly to Tampa to sing at Cecil Todd's Bicentennial Rally. It happened again: the fog "socked us in" at the Lubbock airport, and then came sleet and snow. Some "good Samaritans" from Tulsa, Oklahoma, flew me to Dallas in a Lear jet, where I would change to another plane for Tampa. This was my first ride in a Lear jet, and I hope it will not be my last. What an experience! Like a long, gray goose, it zoomed up with lightning speed through the fog and storm into the great, white clouds far above. Talk about mounting up as with the wings of the eagle (*see* Isaiah 40:31)—this was *it.* Got to bed at 2:30 A.M.

Cecil Todd is one of God's greatest. He "tells it as it is." He told so well about the strengths and weaknesses of our country, at this rally, that I wanted to stand up and cheer loudly and long, and he made me bow my head in thankful prayer to the One who has lifted our United States to a high place and blessed her among the nations of the world. Cecil made it clear that this country could be only as great as its people are great, and it will remain great only so long as its people stand fast in their faith in God.

The rally confirmed my faith that we are engaged in a struggle to hold that faith. It is a struggle for survival, and nothing less. It is a struggle not just between differing men, or between conflicting ideologies; it is a struggle against "the prince of the power of the air"—Satan (Ephesians 2:2). Satan is a roaring lion seeking whom he may devour—and he is a strong, insidious foe working within the heart of the nation to corrupt our faith in God, Christ, His Word, and His Spirit.

The chips are down, God's enemies are many and mighty, but God will confound them. In the end He will hold them in derision—as Psalms 2:4 puts it, "He that sitteth in the heavens shall laugh." We Christians may have to undergo real persecution if we stand for Him, but we are told to "endure hardness, as a good soldier of Jesus Christ" (2 Timothy 2:3). The bearing of this cross may be hard for us, but bearing it is a privilege and a duty and not an accident. That cross is very real to me. My God is a very real God, living in my soul, and I will fight it through for Him, and I am strengthened for the fight by the words of Jesus in Matthew 10:28: "And fear not them which kill the body, but are not able to kill the soul."

Someday, this coat of flesh is going to fall apart, anyway, and my soul will wing its way to realms brighter than the sun. So let them call me a fanatic, a fool, a show-business has-been. What does that matter, really? This world is not my home; I have a continuing city to live in (*see* Hebrews 13:14). Hallelujah!

Lest I forget it—a good friend has given me a copy of a little book called *I'm Out to Change My World,* by Ann Kiemel. Ann is only twenty-seven years old, but she writes the way a veteran does and sings a gospel song as an operatic soprano would. Get it and read it. As Lawrence Welk says, it is "wunnerful, wunnerful."

En Route to Waco, Texas

Lord, only You can know the pain that is within me on this plane bound for Baylor University in Waco—leaving my mother again for three days. There is an outbreak of a flu epidemic in her convalescent hospital. She felt feverish when I kissed her last night, and in the morning she had laryngitis. She said she felt so poorly that she didn't even watch Rex Humbard on her TV—and she *never* misses Rex.

Roy promised to stand by and let me know if she gets into trouble.

Now Lord, You have said, "He that loveth father or mother more than me is not worthy of me" (Matthew 10:37). I know what You mean. I know that spreading Thy Word is first priority for my life, and I will go where and when You think I should go. But Lord—You know how Mom looks to me to attend to her business and personal needs, and I am so afraid, many times, that I may be away when You call her home. In the past, You have ordered events, ordered my comings and my goings, and I know I can trust You to be with her. But Lord—I want to be there, too. You know how much I love her and how much I long to shield her from anxiety and suffering.

Yesterday she said to me, "Dale, I was so short of breath that I could hardly eat my breakfast," and she was suffering so with nausea that the doctor had to give her a shot. That tired old heart is faithful but struggling so, even with the pacemaker.

If Mom is hit by the flu, I fear for her survival. But You know what will happen, even as I write this. Please, Father, give her peace and Your blessed assurance, and let her know that I am with her, too, in spirit, and that if she and You want it I will cancel these engagements in Waco and Jacksonville, and get someone else to take my place.

It is strange, Father, how flying away up here in the clouds helps me to get things in focus. The earth below, the squares of land neatly laid out and fenced off, even the mountains are quite small from this distance, and it all makes me see how small our troubles must seem to the Creator!

How come it takes me so long to get around to that truth as I stew in my problems?

The plane is landing. Be with me now, Lord, and may I be with You all through this troublesome day.

Waco, Texas

The craziest things happen to me. Sometimes I think the Lord lets them happen just to keep me humble. I was thinking the other day about a "happening" that hit me as we were flying into Denver. I had come beautifully prepared for my appearance there, with a beautiful pair of beige kid pumps that matched a clutch purse; I was sure that I would look beautiful in that beige getup. I had the shoes packed in my navy blue carryon, which also contained a small bottle of blue cleansing oil. Lo and behold, when I unpacked, I found that the cap had come off the bottle and the contents had spilled all over the lovely beige pumps. I lifted the shoes out carefully—thereby staining my fingers blue, too—and as I looked at the oily mess I wanted to jump up and down and yell like Rumpelstiltskin.

Fortunately, I had an extra pair of dress shoes I had thrown into the bag at the last moment. I was muttering to myself like a spoiled little girl as I put them on, and almost pressed the panic button—almost, but not quite. As I simmered down I thanked my Lord for providing me with a way out of my silly situation. I shut my eyes and said to Dale Evans, "Don't forget, lady, that He always leaves a door open, a way out of every circumstance and crisis."

"In all thy ways acknowledge him, and he shall direct thy paths" (Proverbs 3:6). Amen.

Then there was the crazy hassle at the Waco airport yesterday. I got in at 9:05 P.M., and there wasn't a soul to meet me. I didn't know the name of my contact—someone from Baylor University, where I was to speak. I didn't know *anybody* at Baylor, and I ran around the airport like a chicken with its head off, trying to find somebody who *did* know someone at Baylor. I didn't know where I was to spend the night; maybe I'd have to sleep in the airport lounge! All I knew was "chapel at the university at 10:00 A.M."

I was just about ready to throw in the towel when a young fellow at an airline-ticket counter came to me and said, "Mrs. Rogers, I am a law student at Baylor, and I think the man you are looking for is Dean Wimpy. I'll call him for you."

In fifteen minutes Dr. Wimpy appeared, and drove me to my hotel. Somehow my flight information had never reached him, and he had been on pins and needles all day; this was Sunday, so he had no way of reaching my agency on the West Coast, which was closed for the day.

It all turned out beautifully. My young cousin, Melody Raines, is a student at Baylor; she told me that the audience would be mostly freshmen and sophomores, and they were, and what a fine crowd they were! Dr. Wimpy informed me that I had twenty-eight minutes to speak, but not to worry about it. I didn't. I'm from Texas, you know, and Roy says, "You can always tell a Texan, but you can't tell him much." Texans love to talk, and I am no exception, especially when I get excited about my subject. Since my subject was—and always is—Jesus, it is hard for me to put the stopwatch on Him. We had a great time at Baylor, and I am leaving to fly to Jacksonville, Florida, to speak at the Laymen's Try God Crusade at the coliseum.

Jacksonville, Florida

Everything seemed sunshine and roses as I tripped up the platform steps at the coliseum—and then, halfway up, I caught my heel in my long, gray, taffeta petticoat. If it hadn't been for the help of the escorting sheriff, I'd have taken a bad spill. I got to my seat in the front row with the choir, and I know my face was as red as an overripe beet. The mayor of the town introduced me and I sang some of the songs in my *Heart of the Country* album, and talked (I hope) for only twenty-five minutes.

I sat down and looked at my feet—and saw six inches of my petticoat hanging out in full view of the whole coliseum. The waist clasp had torn loose when I stumbled. I asked a lady sitting behind me to dig for the waistband and reclasp it, and I tried to hide her movements by moving my arms around like a rejuvenated scarecrow. She couldn't reach the clasp, so she took a hat pin and bunched the whole thing together on my hip.

While I fumbled around and tried to look nonchalant, I looked straight into the lens of a TV camera with a man grinning behind it. I mouthed, silently, "Please don't photograph me this way." He laughed and shut off his camera. At the end of the service several woman formed a circle around me and I let the whole petticoat slip to the floor. Fortunately, my skirt was of thick blue serge. I learn something on every trip.

Thank You, Lord, for those dear folks in wheelchairs at the coliseum. They were a blessed inspiration.

San Jose and San Francisco, California

My brother Hillman said to me once, "Sis, it looks as though the old, sad cat is following you." Well, that old cat has caught up with me, in the past few days.

I was just starting out to visit Tom and his family in San Jose; they were to drive me to San Francisco, where I was to do a whole day of promotion for my book *Let Freedom Ring*—TV, newspaper, radio, the whole bit. Halfway between Apple Valley and the Los Angeles airport, I felt the wind blowing my little Toyota Corona station wagon all over the road. It got worse and worse, and I suddenly realized that I couldn't keep the car from pulling to the right. I got out and looked at the tires and sure enough, the rear right tire was flat. My fresh hairdo was flying in the wind, and my first impulse was to finish it off by pulling it apart and throwing sand on my head. Cars whizzed by me, and their drivers didn't even glance at me. (I swore then and there that I would never do that!) I sat there and said, "Lord, You know that tire is flat and You know I can't change it, so I guess it's up to You to send someone along to help me."

The words were hardly out of my mouth when a lady pulled in behind me and asked with a smile, "Can I help?" I wanted to kiss her. She drove on into the next town, and twenty minutes later a service truck reached me.

I had a great time with Tom, Barbara, and Mindy (my eldest grandchild), her husband Jon, Amy (my first great-grandchild), and Julie, Tom's youngest and now a senior in high school preparing to enter the Bible Institute in Los Angeles next fall. Tom and Barbara drove me to San Francisco.

The old cat caught up with me in the lobby of the hotel

in San Francisco. The doorman carried my valet-pack in from the car, and all of a sudden he wasn't carrying it; the handle broke off on one end, and the whole thing fell on the floor with a dull thud. I was fit to be tied; I had no time to purchase a new valet-pack, and I had to have those clothes.

Almost before I knew what was going on, the hotel engineer came and bolted the loose end of the handle to the bag. He wouldn't take a cent for his services. (I must send him one of my books when I get home.)

The schedule in San Francisco was tight, but I got through the luncheon, the long taped interview, the taking of photographs, and the radio talk show. I was more than tired when it occurred to me that I had neglected to pack two whole dresser drawers of personal belongings when I left the hotel for the airport. Phoned the hotel; my things would be sent COD to Apple Valley. I felt like a clobberhead.

Meridian, Mississippi

Arrived in Dallas at 9:45 P.M.; I spent the night at the Airport Marina Hotel, then boarded a plane for Meridian, Mississippi. Taxied out for the takeoff; the traffic was snarled due to thunderstorms. When the pilot revved his motors after a forty-five-minute delay, there were two sharp, gunlike reports; we got off the plane while the pilot took it out to "blow out the engines," to determine the trouble. Compressor out. Lovely! I was two hours late, and already overdue for the evangelical crusade to be conducted by Dr. E.J. Daniels at Meridian. What to do now? There was another plane leaving in thirty minutes, but it would never get me to Meridian in time. Should I call Dr. Daniels and tell him I would be on that plane, or what? Thought I should. I was just dialing Meridian when I heard over the loudspeaker that our engine was okay, and we should board immediately. Good! I would have to change clothes in the plane's rest room. Figured I would arrive in Meridian fully dressed, and be whisked to the crusade.

We were miles up in the air when the pilot announced, "Please keep your seat belts fastened, ladies and gentlemen. There will be no refreshments served. We are flying into a pretty severe thunderstorm. We shall do our best, but it's probably going to be a little choppy." That was the understatement of the century!

As we neared the Meridian airport, the thunder was so loud that I could hear it above the racket of the jet engines, and the lightning flashes lit up the whole inside of the plane. The pilot said, "Sorry, folks, but it is impossible for us to land. We will circle for a while." We circled, we bumped, we lurched, and finally we came down through a downpour that looked like a South Vietnam monsoon. Landed at 6:45 P.M.; the crusade was to commence in fifteen minutes! There was a group of loyal greeters on hand. The mayor presented me with the keys to the city, a lovely lady presented a bouquet of red roses, and we roared off in cars for the auditorium. Wow!

The auditorium had a metal roof.

We were told at the airport that lightning had struck the airport transformer, knocking out the airstrip landing lights, and that was why we had to circle for more than twenty minutes, until they got the lights on again. One couple parted company for the rest of the flight to Atlanta. The terrified wife refused to get back on the plane and rented a car to finish her journey; her husband got back on the plane, and that was that!

At the auditorium I scrambled into a long dress in a trailer, while the song service inside was extended; when I got to the microphone, I could hardly hear my own voice. The downpour on that metal roof was really something—and I was being televised! I began my talk with the words "I can sympathize with those poor folks who got caught in the Great Flood." (I had to get up early the next morning to retelevise my part of the service on tape, because of the ruined sound tracks. But I'm not complaining; most of the sound tracks for most of my engagements have been good on the first try. Into every life some rain must fall, but Lord— *that much?*)

On stage, Dr. Daniels whispered in my ear, "Dale, did you bring all this rain?" Could be, could be. We got to laughing about a similar happening three years earlier, down in Tennessee; it happened in his huge gospel tent. With something like nine thousand people inside and outside the tent, a roaring thunderstorm burst on their poor heads and lightning knocked out the whole sound system before I could be introduced. I don't know— maybe the good Lord was trying to tell me *not* to speak, on both occasions. Humanly speaking, I would like to know who was speaking in those storms —the Lord, or Beelzebub.

We once had a visitor in Apple Valley who said to me, "Sister Rogers, the Lord gave me a message for you; He said for you to be silent and let Brother Rogers speak." Looking back, I think he was right. But just the same, I spoke in Meridian, and we had a good time in the Lord, so it must have been Him telling me to stonewall it against all that rain and thunder.

In one of my interviews, a woman challenged me with this: "Of course, I do not believe in Original Sin, as you do. . . ." It stopped me cold, for a few seconds, for such a statement clearly nullifies the need for the Saviour and His cross. Inwardly, I prayed for a true and gentle answer, and it came: "Nicodemus, a brilliant scholar of the Sanhedrin and well versed in the law and the writings of the prophets, asked Jesus to explain His teaching of Original Sin and of being born again; Jesus told Nicodemus that he *must* be born again, in the Spirit. That implies that we are all born the first time, in the flesh, in a state of spiritual blight, and that there must come a second spiritual birth and baptism if we are to be saved."

The interviewer said that to her it was impossible for a little, innocent baby to be born in sin. I did my best to explain the difference between the two births, but she went away unconvinced. You'll have to take it from there, Lord. This woman is very, very bright, intellectually, and only You and Your Holy Spirit can get through to her. Help her to submit herself to You, and to find a new life, a new heart, and a new intellect. What I couldn't do, You will.

En Route From Yakima, Washington

We had a magnificent time in Yakima, at the Kroese Brothers Crusade. We have just left there; the weather is bad. We have to make some unexpected stops before reaching Los Angeles. Give me patience, Lord.

As I boarded the plane I was thinking of Howard Hughes and the commotion over his "true will." Years ago, I attended a dinner party at which Hughes was a guest; he was a man with a brilliant mind but an apparently loveless life, cursed with an inordinate fear of disease and death; but he was also a wizard in the field of aviation and electronics who had built an incredible industrial empire.

I had been anxious to meet him, but when he arrived I was shocked. Tall, gaunt, dressed in a drab, gray, wrinkled, baggy suit, string tie, and tennis shoes—I couldn't believe my eyes. His words were few and far between, to say the least, and I lost count of the dishes of ice cream they served him. That's all he ate—just ice cream. No wonder his health went from bad to worse. Poor man, with all his wealth and power, he seemed the most unhappy man I had ever met. Actually, he was poor in the things that count, for true riches are to be found not in banks but in the Spirit and in the love and company of family and friends. Jesus said that he who would save his own life would lose it. Hughes seemed to have lost everything, long before he died.

Home

Oh, my aching heart. It has happened. She is gone, my wonderful little mom.

Two months ago, back in March, Tom invited me to be with him in his production of Handel's *Elijah,* at the Calvary Baptist Church in Los Gatos, California. While I had determined to cut down on my traveling schedule and spend more time with Mom, I couldn't turn that one down. So I spent Saturday afternoon of the first of May with her before taking off for Los Gatos at 5:15 P.M. She said to me, "Honey, I will miss you, but I'm so glad you will be with Tom. You are not together nearly enough, so go." Tom had been the apple of her eye all her life, and she had a great part in raising him. As I bent to kiss her forehead on leaving, I had a strong compulsion to stay with her and "pray it through," to ask God to forgive any concealed bitterness or disappointment in either of us, but she insisted that I be with Tom that day. So I thanked Him for letting me have her these sixty-three years, for the beautiful example of Christian living that she had been to me and to so many others, and asked Him to relieve her of any anxiety for me as I traveled. I placed both of us squarely in His hands, knowing that only good could come from those hands. I thanked Him for His watchful care over her, and for the kindness of the people at the nursing home. As I finished she said, "Thank you, honey; kiss Tom and his family for me." I blew her another kiss from the door and blithely promised, "I'll call you tonight and you can talk with the whole family, and on Monday I'll give you a full report on Tom's *Elijah.*"

There were no misgivings on my part about leaving her; she seemed to be the same as she had been for the past two weeks—some bad days, some good ones when she was her old self. And there were plenty of friends who promised to visit her while I was gone.

We called her from Los Gatos at 8:00 P.M. on Saturday, and everyone talked with her. Barbara, my daughter-in-law, commented that Mom seemed tired and weak. I was so accustomed to seeing her that way that it was not noticeable to me. Strange, isn't it, how we drift unknowingly into acceptance of the inevitable—and how God prepares us for it? The doctor had not promised me that Mom would ever be strong again, after her heart arrest and the installment of the pacemaker—nor did he tell me how precarious the situation might be; he just said that she was a tired little old lady with a weak heart and a pacemaker.

Perhaps I expected too much from an eighty-six-year-old heart that had endured two cataract operations, a broken hip, a breast-cancer removal, and the death of her only son, Hillman, all within a space of four years. So many times she had said, during those years, "I am so tired; I wish the Lord would take me in my sleep," to which I would say, "Mom, don't talk that way. You'll probably outlive me." Once she replied to that, "If you don't slow down, you'll never make it to eighty-six!" Secretly, I prayed that the Lord would take her first, so that she wouldn't have the added heartbreak of losing me, her only daughter and remaining child.

On Sunday at *Elijah,* my heart sang with praise and thanksgiving to God for such incredibly lovely music. The huge choir and orchestra, the soloists, the depiction of Elijah on the mount challenging Ahab and the followers of Baal, the blazing altar fire from a back-lighted screen—perfect! As I watched my son lift his arms and draw that marvelous music from the cast, I thought, "Oh, if only Mom could see the fruits of her labors in her grandson!" Tears came as the entire congregation jumped to its feet in a long standing ovation. Tom was exhausted and dripping with perspiration in the car on the way back to his home.

As we entered the house, there was a long, insistent ringing of the telephone. When I answered it, the operator was saying, urgently, "Long distance for Tom. . . . Long distance for Tom." I thought that was odd—his name was Tom Fox; why? Tom took the receiver and listened for a moment, and then his face blanched. I heard him ask, "When did it happen?" I grabbed the receiver from him, for I knew. . . . The choked voice of my good friend Judy said, "Dale, Mom has gone into congestive heart failure; come as quickly as you can."

My face covered with tears, I asked Tom to call the airport. There was a plane due to leave in forty-five minutes. As Tom packed his bag, I dialed my mother's private phone, by her bed. Judy answered it, and I asked her if she had told me the whole story. Was Mom still alive and conscious? She put Mom on the phone; gasping and choking, she managed a weak hello. Fighting to keep my voice steady, I begged her, "Mom, I love you so much. Tom and I are on our way; please hold on for us." She managed a weak "All right. . . ."

As Tom and I went up the steps into the plane in San Jose, she drew her last breath. It was 9:00 P.M.

The flight home took an hour, and we raced in our car up El Cajon Pass to Victorville: the speedometer said eighty most of the way, and I hoped for a highway patrolman to stop us and give us an escort that could move us even faster. As we pulled to the curb in front of the hospital, I saw our pastor, Bill Hansen, with Judy Atherton and Dusty and a nurse walking out the door. I shouted, "We're not too late, not too late?" I knew we were. I flew into Mother's room to her empty bed, put my head down on the pillow, and cried my eyes out.

The Lord has not permitted me to witness the passing of any of my children, my brother, my dad, or my mother. I'm sure there are some who would resent that, but I do not. I know He has a very good reason for this, and I do not question Him.

Thinking back in the past week, I now realize that Mom had been slowly receding from us. Had I known, I most certainly would not have gone to Los Gatos—and I know that the Lord knew this and that He allowed me to go, for His own reasons. My secretary, Bernice, was very fond of Mom and visited her often. She had been with her on Saturday, after I had left, and Mom said to her, "I guess I won't get to go to the Uvalde Centennial with Frances, but how I would love to go back to Texas, just once more. I guess the only way I will go will be for the last time."

Mrs. Bird, a fine Christian lady, brought Mom a fresh carnation on Saturday morning, and she and Mom prayed (as they had prayed together every Saturday morning) that if Mom could never be on her feet again, the Lord would take her home. Thank You, Lord, for answering their prayers. Mom did not want to be a helpless invalid. Neither did I want her to be one! In Your infinite compassion, You have spared us that, and I am grateful.

Roy had stopped in to see Mom at 7:00 P.M. on Sunday, on his way to the airport to board a plane for Cincinnati. He said her hands and arms were cold, and she seemed exhausted—more than usual—and that she lay with her eyes half-closed. She loved Roy as a son, and she took the place of his mother, who died years ago. When he kissed her good-bye she said, "Good-bye, Roy, I am so tired." And while she didn't say the same thing to her other visitors, they sensed something unusual about her. Bernice is sure that Mom knew she was near the end, and Judy said Mom was very quiet, and somehow different. In the middle of the afternoon on Sunday, Judy asked the nurse if she shouldn't call me, and the nurse said no, that Mom's vital signs were fine. Judy went home for a sandwich around 7:00 P.M., but halfway through her meal she heard a voice saying, "Go back. Go to Mom; she needs you!" She ran back to the nursing home to find the nurses working feverishly over Mom, who was breathing heavily. The nurse told Judy to call me at once.

All the way from Victorville to Los Angeles, Roy couldn't get Mom off his mind. The minute he checked in at the motel at the airport, he called the hospital desk—and learned that she had just gone.

Now, the first shock over, God reached down and wiped the tears from my eyes and lifted me up to do what had to be done. His Spirit whispered to me, "Accept it!" and accept it I did. Could I give one word of advice to those who lose a loved one? *Accept it!* The sooner you do that, the sooner the pain will leave your heart. God is no fool. He knows what He is doing, when He takes one from us. Give God a chance to heal your wound.

I did just that, and I felt as though He had laid a cool hand on my brow, and a surge of strength ran through me. Time and time again, it has happened to me; in times of temptation or near despair or severe emotional trauma, I have turned to Him and He has opened a gateway of escape—into Himself, where abide the peace and strength which surpass all human understanding. Only those who have experienced the resurrection power of Christ in their lives can comprehend the endurance of the Christian in times such as these.

I insisted that Roy go on to Cincinnati and keep his engagement there; it was too late for him to break the date. Tom and I made all the arrangements for the funeral service in Victorville: the flight to Texas, another service in Central Baptist Church in the town of Italy, and the interment beside my dad in Hillcrest Cemetery in Waxahachie.

I looked at her just before the service began in Victorville. She looked every bit the angel she had been in her life, in a pink-and-gray dress I had bought for her four years ago. I was glad, behind the tears of parting, that my beloved Bettie Sue Smith was at last free in that blessed realm of rest and joy in the Lord. This was, I think, the greatest triumph of my life.

The Spirit moved in that room, comforting all of us! Pastor Bill Hansen was magnificent; the Spirit put words upon his lips that not only comforted but also inspired all of us. As he spoke, I found myself saying, "Just think, Mom—you have had two graduation services—one from college and now this one into heaven." Death, to me, is a commencement, the ending of a merely human life and the commencing of another, far better life. "Praise the Lord, praise the Lord, let the people rejoice." Yes, *rejoice!* That's what God's Book says, and I do rejoice.

Then came the flight to Texas. We ran into another thunderstorm, wild wind and rain, and I prayed, "Oh, Lord, not now. Not today. This is Mom's homecoming. Please let the sun shine for her services." He heard me. It rained most of the night and it was still cloudy and misty the next morning, but at exactly 11:00 A.M. His glorious sunshine broke upon us.

The service in the church was lovely, and Pastor Van Gauthe's little talk was beautiful. He used an illustrative story I think I shall never forget; he told the story of a little boy living in the days of the old river steamboats. It was customary for the townspeople to stand on the banks of the river and wave to the passengers as the boat went by. This lad ran out to the end of the pier, waving and shouting for the boat to turn in and pick him up. The people laughed and told him it was no use; that boat wasn't going to pull us to the pier for a youngster such as him! The boy turned to them and said, "Oh, yes, it will. My father is the captain of that boat, and he's going to take me to a new home up the river." The people were very quiet as the huge boat turned toward the shore. I listened, and I thought of Mom, in her new home, and I was glad.

A young woman in Mom's church sang "I Need Thee Every Hour" and sang it well. Tom said it took him back to the days of his childhood with her, when he stood at her side and sang the hymn with her. Then Theiss Jones (one of the Century Men and an old, dear friend) sang her favorite hymn, "He Touched Me," in such triumph of Spirit that I wanted to shout, "Yes, He touched her and made her whole life beautiful, and now she is no longer ill, needs no more medicine, no more shots—nothing, for she has everything in Christ."

It was pretty difficult to look upon the earthly tabernacle of her departed spirit for the last time, and it was terribly hard for Roy. How he loved her! It is something for a husband to ask his wife to send for her mother to come to his house because he misses her! Actually, when he and I had disagreements, Mom usually sided with Roy. I used to accuse her of being partial to boys. I shall forever be grateful to Roy for his love and kindness to my mother.

At the cemetery, as the pastor read the Twenty-Third Psalm, and as I looked at Mom's casket, the Lord did something beautiful to me. He convinced me that, so far as I was concerned, I had no relation whatever with that physical body they were laying to rest. Mom was free in the heavenlies, and I sensed that freedom and joy for her in the deepest recesses of my heart.

Incidentally, it rained all night after the funeral, and all the next day, as Roy, Tom, and Barbara returned to California and I went about the sad work of taking care of Mother's business and her will with the attorney and the tax man.

The condolences that came to me from my friends did

much to lift me out of my sorrow. A good friend of mine and an illustrious lady of law and letters, Mrs. Kemper Campbell, wrote me, "One thought comforts us—where they have gone, we are going forever. The weariest river flows at last into the sea." I love that. And I love the words sent by Paul Evans, a brother of Louis Evans, Sr., and an active member of our church in Apple Valley: "When my father died some years ago, a great man of God, Homer Rodeheaver, sent us this comforting message: 'Death is but a starlit strip between the communion of today and the reunion of tomorrow.' I sometimes think that our sorrow and tears are a sort of interest we pay on the loan of these dear ones God has let us have for a while." Bless him!

I asked Bill Hansen, our pastor, to tell me about Mom's passing, since only he and Judy were with her at the time. He said that Judy called him just before he was about to leave for Palm Springs. God's timing was perfect. When he arrived at the hospital he found Judy holding my mother's hand, praying, tears spilling down her cheeks. She had told Mom I was coming, and she was trying to keep her awake. Mom lay as if asleep. Bill patted her cheek and said to her, "Bettie, this is Bill; we are going to pray." No response from Mom. He held one of her hands, Judy held the other. After he prayed, he started to read the Twenty-Third Psalm. Just as he read, "He leadeth me beside the still waters" (verse 2), Mom turned toward him, opened her eyes, looked him full in the face, closed her eyes again, took a few shallow breaths

—and was gone. Bill said her passing was one of the most beautiful and peaceful he had ever witnessed.

"Precious in the sight of the Lord is the death of his saints" (Psalms 116:15).

Memphis, Tennessee

The worst thing we can do, when loved ones leave us, is to stay in the house and just feel sorry for ourselves, or to ask God over and over, "Why does this have to happen to me?" Let them go, give them into God's hands and get out of that house and get busy about your Father's business, just as soon as you can. That way lies healing. Take it from an old veteran of trials and tears—I have found that this is the way out.

The Sunday after the funeral, I witnessed and sang at two crusades in West and East Memphis with evangelist Jerry Spencer. I found rare comfort in visiting with my cousins in Memphis and in renewing old friendships. Memories came in a great flood in this city that had given me my start in radio long, long ago. I thought of the times when my family was there—when Tom was a baby—when I worked (not for long!) as a secretary—when we used to troop out to attend services at the Bellvue Baptist Church, across the street from our home. Now just Tom and I are left.

I stood on the balcony of the hotel and looked out over the friendly city and at that old river, the Mississippi, "jest keeps rollin' along." I thought to myself, *What a lot of water has gone under the bridge, in my life; so much water, such joys and such sorrows, and it keeps right on rolling along.* No sorrow, no joy, has brought an end to life; it just keeps rolling, moving, flowing, as though the Creator never meant it to stop but to go on forever. Life goes on; we bandage our wounds, get up, and get back in the battle.

Only two of us are left, yes, but there is so much for us to do! I picked up my Living Bible and read Hebrews 12:12,13: "So take a new grip with your tired hands, stand firm on your shaky legs, and mark out a straight, smooth path for your feet so that those who follow you, though weak and lame, will not fall and hurt themselves, but become strong."

This one thing shall I do, come what may.

En Route Home

I keep thinking about my moving around so much, day after day and year after year. I think I move because I *must* move. It isn't in me to sit still and wait until someone else moves out for Christ.

My good friend and pastor, Larry White, told me a good story about this the other day. It was a story about Corrie ten Boom, who is a "tramp for the Lord" all over the world. She's even more lively than I am. It seems that Corrie was about to address a group of people whom she called "Let the Lord do it" Christians—people who can never get around to operating on time. They were sitting and standing around the room, some of them praying and most of them just talking and waiting for someone to get things going. Corrie waited and waited. When she could wait no longer she said to them, "God expects us to wait upon Him, and I often wait for His guidance, but I don't believe He is going to move these chairs into place for us to begin the program." Then they moved.

Amen, Corrie, and right on! Yes, the Lord does give guidance, but He also speaks out against sloth and laziness. Think of the words of Jesus to the man He had just healed of paralysis: "Take up thy bed and walk" (John 5:11). To the man with the withered hand He said: "Stretch forth thine hand" (Matthew 12:13). Too often we Christians sit around bemoaning our misfortunes, expecting the Lord to start things going right again by a miracle. He expects us to do something about it, to move out and work out His will in our lives and in the lives of others.

Get going, Christian!

Home

I wore a white flower for Mom this Mother's Day. Roy knew what I was going through, and he was sweet to me. After church we had lunch with Judy Atherton, her son Ralph, and his family. In the afternoon Dusty came over with his family, Marion with hers, then Dodie and Nikki. That helped more than those dear kids can ever know. But still, it was a difficult day. They left us at just about the time

I had for so long left the house to visit Mom. Roy saw the tears gathering and mercifully suggested that we go for a ride and let it out. That is the thing to do in a situation such as this. We are wrong to try *not* to cry—tears are part of God's therapy.

Sometimes we call it "the merry, merry month of May." It hadn't been merry for me, but still, there had been a few light spots to relieve the tension and the tears—for example, the experience with the parking-lot attendant at the Inglewood, California, airport, on my way back from Memphis. These poor, harassed fellows who park your car when you leave it and find it for you when you come back need all the smiles they can get. I know a lot of easier ways to earn a living. I imagine that they have a lot of trouble with people who complain about the cost of parking, or maybe it's those impatient people who are always in such a hurry to leave the lot.

I had dealt with this fellow before; he had a rough, tough, hurry-up manner and a gruff voice. Actually, he was inclined to tease his customers a little, as if to say, "Come on, come on, I haven't got all day!" He bellowed that at me as I dug a twenty-dollar bill out of my purse. As he handed me the change, it was a dollar too much, and I asked, timidly, "Are you sure you haven't given me a dollar too much?"

He scowled the blackest scowl I have ever seen; then he looked at his ticket, scratched his head, and looked back at me as though he just couldn't believe it. He actually smiled.

"Say, you know you're a good girl?" (He used the word *girl* loosely.)

"I'm a Christian," I said.

That flustered him; he sputtered a bit and then blurted out, "Well, I wish more. . . . Anyhow, have a good day!"

I wish I'd had a testimony tract to give him. Maybe next time. . . .

Soon after the death of my mother, I once more became a great-grandmother. Candi (Tom's daughter) and her husband, Todd Halberg, had given me an eight-pound, twelve-ounce baby girl at the Presbyterian Hospital in Whittier, California. I stopped off at Art Rush's home to ask about Candi. All of us were worried about her diabetic condition during pregnancy. Mary Jo, Art's wife, told me that Candi was fine, but the baby had problems, and they were testing her for Down's syndrome. The baby, named Bethany Ann, was having difficulty breathing and had fluid in her lungs, blueness in her legs, and a spreading jaundice in her stomach. There was also speculation about a rare blood disorder which kept the blood cells from reproducing properly. She had had two transfusions, which didn't seem to help.

I saw the real peace of God in both Candi and Todd; they realized what was involved. Candi prayed that she might have no bitterness in her heart if she lost Bethany; in great humility she said, "She is God's; we are trusting Him." They were both magnificent in their faith.

I went to see Bethany in the Pediatrics Intensive Care

Unit; I looked through the glass window and in choking sorrow said to myself, "Shades of little Robin!" She lay under a shield with a bright light upon her, with pads on her eyes and tubes protruding from her stomach. She was struggling, struggling for life.

On the following Saturday I had to leave for Buffalo, Minnesota, near Minneapolis, to keep an engagement for two concerts with the Blackwood Singers. If ever I did *not* want to go anywhere, it was then. But I went; at the concerts, there were prayers for Bethany Ann.

On Friday evening the doctors had told Todd and Candi that Bethany's condition was becoming critical. Todd and a little group of friends in Christ asked permission to anoint her with oil—an unusual request in Intensive Care, but it was granted. As the attending nurse fanned oxygen into Bethany's face, the men joined hands and asked God to heal her in the flesh, in any way He wished, and then they asked for a real sign in the Spirit that He had heard. Todd said that he felt, almost immediately, a warm glow of assurance, and that he was at peace. When he told Candi in her room, she felt the same glow.

At 11:30 P.M., on Sunday after the second concert in Buffalo, I called Roy; he told me that Bethany had died at 6:00 A.M. that day. This was the Lord's Day, the same day on which Mom had died. His Day, His will, His deep purpose; as though God had placed them there, the words of Romans 8:28 fell from my lips as I hung up the phone: "We know that all things work together for good to them that love God, to them who are the called according to his purpose."

Just recently, at the New Covenant Church in Saint Louis, I recounted some of the miracles in my life. A lady in the audience sent up a note which read, "Miracle—a coincidence where God chooses to remain anonymous." Now I was to see a miracle in the lives of Candi and Todd.

They wanted no funeral or memorial service for Bethany, but only what they called a Praise Service in the Whittier Baptist Church. With an unexpected joy mixed with tears I watched Todd climb onto a stool with his guitar, sit with bowed head as he waited upon the Lord, and then start singing and leading all of us in hymns and songs of praise. Between songs he told us how God had blessed and strengthened his and Candi's faith with the advent and the passing of their baby. He asked Candi, sitting on a nearby sofa, to speak for herself, and she told of how God had blessed her own life in this situation.

This beautiful grandchild of mine told us that she had been an almost lifelong insulin-taking diabetic, and of how she and Todd had understood that having a baby might be risky— but they trusted God. She told of listening to a televised sermon during the last month of her pregnancy, when she had been put to bed because of toxemia and a swelling of her limbs. The minister had said that most Christians need to be broken before they can be really effective in the Master's use; that He used different methods for the breaking: in some instances it was necessary to take a loved one from their midst. Candi thought at first that this, for her, might mean the taking of her beloved husband: "God just couldn't take my *baby!* It's *my* baby." Then it came to her that this was God's baby, and that He could and should do whatever He wanted with that baby.

Then she told of how God and Todd had cushioned the blow for her, how they generated that wonderful peace in the hospital room. There was scarcely a dry eye in the room when she had finished—and scarcely a person whose faith was not strengthened by the witness of these two young Christians. Candi and Todd could not possibly have done this in their own strength. But, as Paul says in Hebrews 11:34: ". . . out of [our] weakness [are we] made strong . . ." and made valiant for the fight. Hallelujah!

Tom and Barbara, Candi's parents, stood solidly behind their child in her crucible testing; not once did either of them ask, "Why, Candi?" In quiet, trusting submission they, too, bowed to God's will.

That took some kind of faith. I salute it!

Bill Hansen says that he has witnessed many passings, but that he has always found the passing of the Christian quite different from that of the nonbeliever. The nonbeliever is usually frantic with resentment and fear, struggling against the inevitable. The believer thoroughly believes that the Lord prepares His own for their departure, and when He beckons they go gladly. For this reason alone I would be a Christian.

The flesh fights for survival from the moment of birth. Only the spirit can accept the death of the flesh.

Home Later

I keep thinking back to the wonderful time I had with the folks at the New Covenant Church in Saint Louis. This church is an abounding, astounding fellowship in Christ—nondenominational, it leaps over every sectarian boundary line and finds a blessed unity in the Spirit. Its growth has been phenomenal. Its pastor, who (like me) came out of a questionable background in his youth, dares to believe that God can bring anyone with such a background to a more noble life with Him, and he is winning many, many of like mind.

I enjoyed my fellowship with these people. They had invited me to feed them, and they fed *me.* They had two services—one at 3:00 P.M. and another at 7:00 P.M. By the time I was through with the first one I was so emotionally and physically drained that I was sure I could never get through the second one. At the hotel, after a quick shower and a bowl of soup, some cottage cheese, and applesauce, I stretched out on the bed for a twenty-minute rest. As I got up from that, I had a dismaying spell of weakness and I prayed, "Lord, take over, I've had it."

When the pastor's wife, Mrs. Beckett, came for me, I literally plopped like a sack of meal on the front seat of her car. I said very little on the way to the "Sheep Shed," as they call their building, too tired for any small talk. As I walked into the pastor's study, three young men took my hands and said, "Let's pray." We prayed, and strength flowed into me like a mighty river. It sustained me through the entire service. How true it is what Isaiah says: "They that wait upon the Lord shall renew their strength; they shall mount up with wings as eagles; they shall run, and not be weary; and they shall walk, and not faint" (Isaiah 40:31).

So I go on walking and running, being exhausted and being strengthened, endlessly. I don't regret one moment of it; I intend to wear out in His service and not rust out.

Du Quoin, Illinois

Roy and I, Dusty, Art Rush, and the Sons of the Pioneers are here in Du Quoin, and we love it. We came here (on the country's two hundredth birthday, the Fourth of July) to take part in a county-fair program, and to give my witness. Driving here from Saint Louis, I found out what the words "America, the Beautiful" and "fields of amber grain" really mean. This is a beautiful "amber grain" country; we drove through great, endless fields of corn and soybeans, topped by a deep blue sky filled with great white clouds which seemed to be chasing each other around in sheer glee. How rich is our country in natural beauty and bountiful soil—and love of freedom!

Those clouds up there, we discovered later that night, had some water to drop on us, and it began dropping as we opened our program. Happily, both the grandstand and the stage were covered, and it didn't dampen the enthusiasm of the crowd for one minute. Saturday night brought more people—and more rain, and I began to worry about a wet Sunday morning, when I was scheduled to speak. Silly girl! When I got out of bed on Sunday I rushed to my bedroom window and saw the world full of sunshine. We had a glorious service with a huge crowd. It was the finest Fourth of July I have ever known.

Later, we watched the TV coverage of the great Tall Ships parade, up the Hudson River. It did things to me. At first I bounced around like a child, oohing and aahing myself almost to exhaustion. But in the quieter moments a tear ran down my cheek. I thought of how my brother Hillman, an air force man, would have enjoyed it, and I thought of Sandy —also an enlisted man—both of them thought it a privilege to serve their country in the armed services. In my mind's eye I saw the little flags waving over their graves, and I was one with the countless mothers, wives, sweethearts, and children of those who had lost their lives in that service. I murmured the words of Paul: "I was born free" (*see* Acts 22:28). How many have died to give us this freedom? It cost us nothing; it cost them their lives.

Speaking of being born—Roy and I watched the five-hour TV program entitled "Hunger"; it was sponsored by World

Vision, the blessed group which put us in touch with little Korean Debbie, long ago. World Vision concentrates on finding homes for destitute—and often illegitimate—babies who were born, seemingly, into a horribly heedless world. My heart almost broke as I watched the shots of those little emaciated, neglected, and love-hungry children. One woman left a baby to die of exposure, and die she certainly would have, but for World Vision workers who picked her up and gave her weeks of tender, loving care. The baby is still alive and gaining in her fight for survival—and waiting for some concerned Christians to come along and adopt her. Working all over the world, World Vision is finding good homes and loving parents who are willing to help. Thank You, Lord!

As we were told by the doctor who delivered our Robin, "Love can do more to help a sick child than anyone or anything else." Love is of God, and God is love, and He and His love are still at work in our world.

En Route to Alberta, Canada

Just had something good happen to me. On my way to the Calgary Stampede, I had to walk, loaded down like a pack mule, the length of the San Francisco Airport. But before I could get started, a public-relations man picked up my bundles and dropped them—and me—in a lovely waiting lounge, where a lovely young hostess took over. She is the widow of a former Pan-Am pilot, working as a volunteer in the lounge, just looking after lonesome travelers such as me. We talked and laughed together until it was boarding time, and we talked about things that mattered, such as sorrow, death, and other trials and troubles. She was radiant in her courage and her faith, and I loved her as a delightful lady who refuses to sit at home feeling sorry for herself and making life miserable for everybody else—including her *nine* children! She brightened my day.

As we were talking, another employee of the airline came through the back door of the lounge and said to me, "I just wanted to meet a fellow Christian, and I wanted you to know that there are plenty of us around."

Put it down in your notebook, Christian: *You never walk alone.* He is always with you on your pilgrimage, and He is always sending His people to cheer you on your way.

Later

Calgary was something. Met some old friends and made some new ones. The worship service at which I spoke was a daring effort made by the Church of the Nazarene at the rodeo. There were cowboys and cowgirls and buckskin horses and a lot of nasty Brahma bulls just waiting for some cowpoke to climb aboard and ride them. A lot of the cowboys came to the service on Sunday morning, along with many of the officials. Many of these cowboys belong to the Christian Athletes organization, and I found that they are men with long spurs on their heels and soft, open, receiving hearts under their shirts. The Lord is really casting His net far, wide, and deep today. Everywhere in Alberta I found dedicated and excited Christians from all walks of life. There's definitely something in the wind: it is the Holy Spirit of God, falling like spring rain on parched fields everywhere—and it's great to be alive and to see it working.

We had a good luncheon before catching the plane home. I was startled and humbled at this luncheon, and a bit embarrassed, when several people came up to me and said, "Your show was great!" I appreciated their compliments—but I hadn't come to put on a show. I had come to witness. I was deeply touched by their standing ovation at the service—and I accepted it as respect for the One I represent as a witness. So long as it is *that,* I am glad—but I want every bit of credit for it to go not to me but to Jesus Christ, for I am nothing without His Spirit dwelling in me and speaking through me.

The more I speak and witness, the more I realize how utterly dependent I am upon the Lord, and the more I feel my personal inadequacy to win anyone to Him.

You know, I am frightened sometimes when I think of those scanning machines they they use today in hospitals and doctors' offices to find tumors and other elements of sickness in the human body. I am frightened, I suppose, at the thought of what they might find. Well, I believe that the Holy Spirit is constantly "scanning" my soul—and I am aghast, many times, at what it could reveal. "Search me, O God, and know my heart: try me, and know my thoughts" (Psalms 139:23).

Tom's two daughters met my plane when it landed in San Francisco and whisked me off to a day of rest and recreation with their family. My weariness fell from me like a pack from a tired mountain climber's back. My little great-grandaughter, Amy Elizabeth, who calls me "Gigi," entertained me with a toy saxophone, nodding her head to keep the beat of her granddaddy, who played an "accompaniment" for her on the piano. Precious gift of laughter—precious gift of children sent to make us laugh off our tiredness! I came home refreshed.

I dashed from the Los Angeles airport to make a reception for Roy and Waylon Jennings at the Palomino Club in North Hollywood, celebrating the opening of *McIntosh and T.J.*

Then I took a good look at my itinerary for the next month, and I almost gave up the ship. There is a short promotional spot to be taped for a Lutheran Hour TV program and the opening of the new Roy Rogers-Dale Evans Museum in Victorville, as starters on a full month of personal appearances. Add to that the telephone that never stops ringing, my attempts at figuring out airplane departures and arrivals, the thousand and one chores to be done around the house, trying to remember birthdays and anniversaries, typing my book notes, working on songs for recording, repairing and adding to the wardrobe—wow! I had thought that by the time I had reached my present age I would be in a rocking chair, rocking quietly, watching the spectacular desert sunsets each day, reflecting on the past and—I would have enough to keep me reflecting until I was one hundred years old!

But it wasn't to be that way at all.

While walking through the corridors of the museum, with its display of memorabilia of our life together, I just stood still and thanked God that it has all been so *good.* I felt not a bit of weariness with it all, but a deep sense of humility. We've been in the public eye most of our lives, and people who live there are very vulnerable figures, but we have survived it all, and on the whole, have done pretty well not just for ourselves but for our Christ as well.

I've often been asked, "Don't you get tired of having people point you out, stare at you, and ask for your autograph? What does it feel like to live in a fishbowl?" Well, sometimes it does get to me, especially when I am tired or not quite up to par. But it is my conviction that when one chooses to live a public life in *any* profession, one should first count the cost of living such a life and not whimper at its pressures. If and when the time comes that I (like Garbo) "Vant to be alone," in anonymity, then I shall retire. In spite of all our good intentions we sometimes become physically fatigued and nervously "on edge," and that tends to make us irritable— and hard to live with! When we get that way, we deserve to be told, "Pardon me, but your image is slipping."

It is difficult to stand on a pedestal. Did you ever try

standing perfectly straight and smiling for just ten minutes? It isn't fun. Sometimes it seems like murder, but we have to do it.

For some years Roy and I participated in the New Year's Day Rose Bowl Parade in Pasadena; all along the route we had to smile, and I used to feel that my face was frozen tight before we reached the end. My cheeks and my jawbone would ache for days after it was over. If I dared to relax for just a minute or so, someone in the bleachers would yell at me, "Hey, what's the matter with you, Dale? You mad about something? Smile!" See what I mean? It isn't always easy to "laugh, clown, laugh," but if you want success in public life, you'd better learn to smile, smile, smile. It's the name of the game.

A superstar said recently, "All I owe the public is my best performance." No, that isn't all he owes the public. He wouldn't have become a star at all without the applause of that public, and he should have the courtesy to thank them for that. We should all be as courteous and as friendly with others as it is in us to be. Stop *whining*.

I look at Jesus and I remind myself of how He endured the crowds that surrounded Him. He was beautifully humble as He said, "Why callest thou me [the human Jesus] good? there is none good but one, that is, God" (Matthew 19:17). He must have been completely exhausted, physically, many times, but He never took His resentment out on the crowds that made Him so weary. Instead, He "went apart," went off alone into the wilderness or up on a mountain, where He could pray and talk with the Father and gain strength from the Father. He never lashed out at the pressing crowd; He simply absented Himself for a while, to be refreshed.

We Christians should follow His example, as we strive to follow Him in spirit.

We should also understand that our finest intentions and even our finest contributions can be wiped out by just one little mistake—and that the same crowd that has placed us on a pedestal can often knock us off the pedestal. Beware of pedestals! In one little moment of weakness or compromise, that can happen, and I think *that* is a sin of the crowd, more than the sin of the image the crowd admires.

I have a beautiful porcelain figure of a mother supporting a young child as he takes his first steps. Some day, in my hurrying clumsiness, I might knock it over and break it, and that would make me cry. If it could be repaired, I would certainly have it repaired. I would not want one moment of carelessness on my part to rob me of my enjoyment of this beautiful piece of art.

Let's face it: we all have feet of clay. Jesus knew that and the Early Church knew it. When a member of the New Testament Church became unruly or fell back into his old sinning ways, he was brought before the church and told that he must confess his misdeeds to the congregation and ask forgiveness of God and the people. Until he was ready to do that, he was deprived of his post in the church, and of its fellowship.

Forgiveness. That's the word! *Forgiveness.* Why do we find it so hard to forgive the mistakes we all make in one form or another? Why can't we forgive and forget the wrong, when it is confessed? Why do we allow one little mistake to ruin the careers and the lives of so many people? After all— which of us is so perfect as to cast the first stone? And who among us, living decently and unselfishly for years, would relish being put on the shelf and denied another chance for just one mistake, however serious it might be?

I don't fear the crowd, but I know how fickle it can be. Both crowd and individual need to cultivate their little gardens of forgiveness, if the wounds of humanity are to be healed and good Christians kept good in spite of occasional error. Only our God of love and forgiveness can help us to do that—the same God who told us that we *must* forgive, if we wish to be forgiven (*see* Luke 6:37). And who doesn't need to be forgiven?

All of this bothers me; I have to resist the temptation to go on and on talking about it. I heard of a tirelessly talking wife who was stopped in the middle of one of her orations by a loving husband who said to her, "Ah, my love, how you *do* run on!" I think I've "run on" about enough. Let me wind it all up with this:

I am sentenced for life to the service of this loving, forgiving, compassionate God in Christ. I know of no better way in which to spend my life than this—to humbly spread the message of His power to heal the trials and troubles of mankind.

I have drunk deeply of the cup of life. I have known days of darkness and of light, hours of tragedy and defeat and blessed moments in which it was all conquered at a wave of His hand and at the sound of His voice saying, as He said to Peter as He walked on the Sea of Galilee, "Be of good cheer; it is I; be not afraid" (Matthew 14:27).

I have heard no other voice with such power and authority and effect. I have found that it is He and He alone who can wipe the tears from my eyes and the grief from my heart and strengthen me to walk tall again in His light and service.

If there is a better way, please tell me. I have yet to discover it.

Trials, tears, and triumphs? I say of it all as Edwin Markham said it:

> Defeat may serve as well as victory
> To shake the soul and let the glory out.
> When the great oak is straining in the wind,
> The boughs drink in new beauty, and the trunk
> Sends down a deeper root on the windward side.
> Only the soul that knows the mighty grief
> Can know the mighty rapture. Sorrows come
> To stretch out spaces in the heart for joy.

This is not my hope. It is my experience—and I pray that it may be yours.